Parents on Your Side

A Teacher's Guide to Creating Positive Relationships With Parents

by Lee Canter and Marlene Canter

Solution Tree

Copyright © 2001, 1991 Solution Tree
(formerly National Educational Service)
304 West Kirkwood Avenue
Bloomington, IN 47404-5131
(812) 336-7700
(800) 733-6786 (toll free)
FAX: (812) 336-7790
email: info@solution-tree.com
www.solution-tree.com

Second Edition May 2001

ISBN 978-1-932127-57-7

Contents

Introduction

Since 1991, when the first edition of *Parents on Your Side* was introduced, there has been a growing effort in schools to involve parents in their children's education. Increasingly, teachers and administrators recognize that parent support can be a key factor in a student's success in school. Parents are in a unique position to offer insight, assistance, backup, and encouragement concerning their children.

Yet, getting parent support is not always easy. Educators continue to explore the best way to involve parents in their efforts. Noted researcher Joyce Epstein[1] suggests that there must be a multifaceted approach. She has identified six important types of involvement between families, schools, and the community. Her work calls for practices that involve:

n   Assisting families with parenting skills

n   Recruiting and training parent volunteers in the schools

n   Involving families in their children's homework and other academic activities

n   Including families on committees and in other school organizations

n   Working with community agencies and businesses to provide resources to parents and strengthen school programs

n   Communicating with families about school programs and student success

It is this last type of parent involvement—communication—that is the focus of this book.

Through effective communication with parents, teachers can have the greatest impact on their day-to-day success with students. With parents on their side, teachers can more effectively manage most academic and behavioral issues that arise. When the most important adults in a child's life are working together, students benefit enormously.

Today more that ever, teachers are finding themselves in situations that require regular communication with parents. The increasing number of charter schools and community-based schools bring more parents into contact with teachers. The use of email offers a convenient tool for teachers to communicate with parents about homework and their children's progress. Voice-mail systems allow parents to call the school at night and hear assignments delivered in the teacher's own voice. Teachers and schools are building websites that describe school events, policies, and class assignments and even allow parents to view student grades on a regular basis. Schools are creating events that bring teachers and parents into more frequent contact. These increased opportunities for parent-teacher interaction, as well as the traditional parent conferences, necessitate that teachers use skill and sensitivity in the way they speak with parents.

The focus of this book is on those communication skills—how to speak with parents, how to listen to them, and how to reach out for their support.

Various changes have been made in this second edition of *Parents on Your Side*. There is greater emphasis on collaboration. We now recognize the need for parents and teachers to combine their knowledge of students' strengths and limitations, then work together to devise an approach that will lead to student success. This revised edition also includes updated references, plus a reorganization of the original material to clarify the strategies you need.

It is our hope that the skills in this book, in combination with your school and community efforts, will lead to greater parent involvement and success for you and your students.

References

[1] Epstein, J. L. (1997, September/October). Six types of school-family-community involvement. *Harvard Education Letter.* [Online]. Available: http://www.edletter.org/past/issues/1997-so/sixtypes.shtml.

Why Teachers Need Parents, and Parents Need Teachers

Teachers need parents because parent involvement has been proven to significantly improve a student's chance for success in school. A parent's influence on both behavior and academic performance can assist you significantly in your educational efforts at school.

Parents need teachers to inspire the way to better involvement in their children's education. Most parents want to get involved, yet some feel that they have no valuable insights to offer or that their involvement is not appropriate or appreciated. Therefore, parents need teachers to reach out to them, elicit their valuable insights, and let them know that their help is greatly appreciated.

The first section of *Parents on Your Side* discusses the need for communication between parents and teachers and examines the ingredients that make such communication effective.

Chapter 1: Why You Need Parents on Your Side
This chapter discusses why communication with parents is valuable for every teacher's repertoire.

Chapter 2: Having an Effective Attitude
This chapter takes a look at attitudes that enable a teacher to effectively communicate with parents.

Chapter 3: Recognizing Roadblocks
This chapter stresses the importance of being aware of teachers' and parents' misconceptions about each other.

Why You Need Parents on Your Side

"Stephanie just doesn't seem to care about school. She rarely does her homework and most of the time she isn't prepared for class. She could be an A student, but she is barely doing C work. I've spoken to her parents. They said they would make sure she starts doing her homework, but they don't follow through."

"Chris was a problem in class all day today—constantly talking back, yelling, and screaming. I tried reaching his mother. She's never at home and she's told me not to call her at work. She doesn't want to be bothered. She said that there's nothing she can do with her son."

"Nothing I've tried has worked with Michael. He just sits there and won't work. Do you know what his mom said when I called her? She said that during the day he was my responsibility. She said that I am the teacher and I should be able to get him to do his work."

Sound familiar? If so, you're not alone. Educators today are expected to teach more and more students with academic and behavior problems, as well as students who are just not motivated to do their best in school. Complicating this situation is the fact that all too often these students have parents who seem unwilling or unable to become involved in their children's education.

Lack of parental support from the parents of Stephanie, Chris, and Michael resulted in their teachers having to handle these situations on their own—with less than positive results. The frustration of these teachers mirrors the frustration of many educators today who attempt to motivate students without the active support of parents.

Teachers speak out for parent involvement.

A 1989 *Instructor* magazine poll asked educators to name the one thing they would like to tell national policymakers about the most effective way to raise student achievement. The answer given most frequently was "more parental involvement." These teachers went on to state that they felt parental involvement was more important than smaller class size, more important than increased control and power for teachers, more important than promoting student responsibility, and more important than decreasing the time students spend watching television.[1]

The *Instructor* poll was supported by the 1996 Phi Delta Kappa/Gallup Poll of teachers, which reported that lack of support from parents is the biggest problem they face in their classrooms.[2]

And a 1993 article in *The New York Times*[3] succinctly sums it up in its title: "What Do Teachers Want Most? Help From Parents."

Clearly, this is in tune with the current nationwide trend to actively recruit parents' support in their children's education. This effort is supported by federal, state, and local programs: *Goals 2000,* for example, sets partnerships between schools, parents, and communities as a voluntary national goal for all schools, and mandates specific practices and programs to grant parental influence as a prerequisite for funding.[4] Such programs are meant to place students at the center of an open and caring three-way communication among parents, school, and community to drive home the same message: School matters for success in life.

Parents are the most important people in a child's life.

Why do teachers and legislators feel parent support is so important? Think about this: Why did you behave in school? Why did you strive to succeed academically? If you were like many others, your parents were an important factor in shaping your attitude toward school.

"In our home we had two rules about school. Rule #1 was: Do what the teacher says, do your best work, and never misbehave. Rule #2 stated that under no circumstances were we ever to break Rule #1. My parents always let us know that they were prepared to do whatever it took to ensure that we succeeded in school. And I knew that they meant it.

"Looking back now, I can see that my parents really empowered my teachers. When my teacher stood in front of the class, my parents were standing symbolically at his side. A request from my teacher was a request from my parents. A demand from my teacher was a demand from my parents. If I got into trouble at school, I got into twice as much trouble at home. My parents never felt that either my teacher or the school was responsible for me. My parents always knew that they themselves were key to my success. They knew that their interest, involvement, and expectations provided the motivation I had to have to achieve my potential.

"Today I'm a teacher, and I know how much more my students could accomplish if I had that kind of support from more of their parents."

You need this kind of commitment from parents today. Parents are the most important people in a child's life. Their love, affection, support, and approval are fundamental needs of all children. And because parents are number one in importance, they are also number one in the ability to influence and motivate their children.

The value of parental involvement and support has been thoroughly studied and evaluated by leading researchers in the educational community.

- A 1986 United States Department of Education study concluded that "the family is critical to success in school." Indeed, the "curriculum of the home" is twice as predictive of academic learning as socioeconomic status . . . (and) parent influence is no less important in the high school years."[5]

- Noted researcher Urie Bronfenbrenner studied a number of educational intervention programs. He concluded that active involvement and support of the family are critical to a child's success in school.[6]

- R. J. Gigliotti and W. B. Brookover studied schools of similar size, geographic locale, and student SES. They found that parent participation was a critical factor in determining the overall effectiveness of the schools, regardless of the economic level of the parents.[7]

- Joyce Epstein of Johns Hopkins University studied teachers who actively sought parent involvement. She found that there were positive changes in student achievement, attitude, and behavior when teachers included parent involvement as part of their regular teaching practices. The students reported that they had a more positive attitude toward school and more regular home-work habits.[8]

■ Anne T. Henderson summarized nearly 50 studies of parent-involvement programs and concluded the following:

➤ Programs designed with strong parental involvement components produced students who performed better than otherwise identical programs that did not strongly involve parents.

➤ Schools that relate well to their communities have student bodies that outperform other schools.

➤ Children whose parents help them at home and stay in touch with schools score higher than children of similar aptitude and family background whose parents are not involved. Schools in which children are failing improve dramatically when parents are called in to help.[9]

It is said that it takes a village to raise a child. There is no doubt that if the educational village—home, school, and community—is involved and supportive, students benefit.

Parents of the new millennium are anything but a homogeneous group. Their numbers include single mothers, single fathers, stepmothers, stepfathers, double-income households, same-sex partners, parents of various cultural or ethnic origins, newly arrived immigrants, parents of different educational backgrounds, the affluent, the middle class, and an ever-increasing number of poverty-level parents.

These parents—and their situations—may differ in many ways, but in spite of their differences they share something significant in common: Each and every one could be a positive factor in shaping the success of a child. Each and every one could provide the motivation that your students need in order to do their best in school. Thus, it is your responsibility as a teacher to do what is in your power to get their support.

An uninvolved parent, justifiably or not, gives a child the message that the child just isn't important enough to warrant close attention. An involved parent, on the other hand, can provide the boost to a student's self-esteem that will lead to greater success in school and a more fulfilling and accomplished adulthood.

You can learn how to involve parents in their child's education.

Parents on Your Side is a step-by-step program developed to help you, the educator, reach out to parents so that your students may get the support they need to succeed in school and, ultimately, in life. The program is based on two important premises:

1. **You can learn how to communicate effectively with parents.**
    There are teachers today who consistently receive support from all kinds of parents in all kinds of situations. We have studied these educators and found that there are common elements critical to their success. In *Parents on Your Side,* you will learn the techniques that effective teachers use to work successfully with parents.

2. **Parents want to support you.**
    The vast majority of your students' parents really do want to be involved. A 1999 Public Agenda and Public Education Network survey of parents of African-American and white students concluded that, regardless of race or ethnicity, the vast majority of parents believe that "kids learn best when their families stress the importance of education, [and that] respect for the value of school begins at home."[10]

    Parents do care about their children and want to provide needed support. In many cases, however, they just don't know what to do—or if they should do it at all. To put it in perspective, only 25 percent of parents report receiving systematic requests or directions from teachers on how they can help their children academically. However, when requested to give additional assistance, over 85 percent of parents immediately responded and were willing to spend at least 15 minutes per day working with their children.[11] In short, when parents are contacted by skilled, trained teachers who communicate effectively, they will respond.

If students are to reach their full potential, they need the support and encouragement of an entire community of concerned, caring adults. That community includes all of us. And it especially includes students' parents. However, not every parent has a positive attitude toward school and education. School can be imposing and intimidating rather than warm and welcoming. It is your job as a teacher to reach out to all parents and to embrace them as partners in their children's education. To do your job effectively, you need to get those parents on your side.

Parents on Your Side will give you the practical skills and confidence you need to get all parents to support your academic, discipline, and homework efforts. You will learn the following:

- How to develop an effective attitude toward parent involvement (Chapter 2).

- How to recognize and move past the roadblocks that stand in your way (Chapter 3).

- What to do before the school year starts (Chapter 4).

- How to plan a productive Back-to-School Night event (Chapter 5).

- How to establish a yearlong positive parent communication program (Chapter 6).

- How to involve parents in their children's homework (Chapter 7).

- How to develop a plan for conducting parent conferences (Chapter 8).

- How to communicate effectively (Chapter 9).

- What to do when problems arise (Chapter 10).

- How to contact a parent about a problem (Chapter 11).

- How to conduct a problem-solving conference (Chapter 12).

- How to use home-school contracts (Chapter 13).

- How to help parents with discipline problems (Chapter 14).

- How to deal with difficult parents (Chapter 15).

- How to make sure that every parent and student feels accomplished by the end of the year (Conclusion).

In Chapter 2, we'll begin by taking a look at the effective attitude shared by teachers who do get parent support.

References

[1] Clapp, B. (1989). The discipline challenge. *Instructor, XCIX*(2), 32–34.

[2] Langdon, Carol A. (1996, November). The third Gallup/Phi Delta Kappa poll of teachers' attitudes toward the public schools. *Phi Delta Kappan, 78*(3), 244–250.

[3] Chira, S. (1993, June 23). What do teachers want most? Help from parents. *The New York Times,* p. 7.

[4] Epstein, J. L. (1995, May). School/family/community partnerships: Caring for the children we share. *Phi Delta Kappan, 76*(9), 701–712.

[5] United States Department of Education. (1986). *What works: Research about teaching and learning.* Washington, DC.

[6] Bronfenbrenner, Urie. (1966). *A report on longitudinal evaluations of pre-school programs. Washington,* DC: Department of Health, Education and Welfare.

[7] Brookover, W. B., & Gigliotti, R. J. (1988). *First teachers: Parental involvement in the public schools.* Alexandria, VA: National School Boards Association.

[8] Epstein, J. L. (1993). *Effects on parents of teacher practices in parental involvement.* Baltimore, MD: Johns Hopkins University Center for Social Organization of Schools.

[9] Henderson, A. (1987). *The evidence continues to grow.* Columbia, MD: National Committee for Citizens in Education.

[10] Farkas, S., & Johnson, J. (1999). Looking at the school: Public agenda asks African-American and white parents about their aspirations and their fears. *Arts Education Policy Review, 100*(4), 24–27.

[11] Gallup, A. (1989). The second Gallup/Phi Delta Kappa survey of public school teacher opinion. *Phi Delta Kappan, 79*(11).

Having an Effective Attitude

The best way to learn how to get parents on your side is from teachers who are already successful at soliciting parental support. In researching this book, we talked to teachers who consistently get the support they need from parents. These teachers may differ greatly in where they teach, how they teach, and whom they teach, but they do not differ at all in their attitude regarding parents.

These teachers share five important qualities, which will be examined in this chapter:

- Effective teachers know they must have the support of parents.

- Effective teachers reach out to parents as essential partners in a child's education.

- Effective teachers demonstrate concern for the child.

- Effective teachers treat parents the way they would want to be treated.

- Effective teachers demonstrate professionalism and confidence.

In other words, effective teachers don't just "get" parents on their side; they have an attitude that enables them to work successfully with parents.

Effective teachers know they must have the support of parents.

Effective teachers understand, without a doubt, that when parents are involved, students do better academically and behaviorally. Experience supports this conclusion. Research backs it up. But effective teachers take this knowledge one step further. As professionals responsible for the education of their students, these teachers believe that it is a dereliction of responsibility to allow a student to flounder academically or behaviorally without doing everything possible to help—and "help" means getting parents involved. Any lesser effort would be, in their view, "educational malpractice."

Effective teachers also unequivocally believe that they owe it to themselves to receive support from parents. Teachers are often faced with the responsibility of not only educating students but of helping solve their emotional and behavioral problems, too. It is not in anyone's best interest to struggle endlessly over student problems without the involvement of parents. It's emotionally draining, time consuming, and, ultimately, nonproductive.

For your students and for yourself, you must have parental support. Parents are in a unique position to deliver the help that is needed.

Effective teachers reach out to parents as essential partners in a child's education.

No one—teacher, principal, counselor, or psychologist—can have as profound an impact on student behavior as can parents. Parents are the most important, influential people in a child's life. Parental love and approval are fundamental needs of every child. All children want and need the praise and positive support of their parents.

And yet, parents may not be aware of the influence they have over their children or how to use this influence to their best advantage. When necessary, you must be prepared to guide parents toward positive reinforcement techniques that will motivate their child to greater success in school.

Parents have the most time and opportunity to give their child individual attention. No matter how dedicated a teacher you are, you have a limited amount of time to work one-on-one with students. For example, in a typical elementary classroom, you may spend a maximum of five minutes per day working with students individually on their reading or math skills. When you can encourage a parent to spend 15 minutes a night helping a child, you are tripling the amount of individual attention that child can receive. Likewise, the one minute of personal attention a secondary teacher may be able to give a student could be increased as much as 15-fold when the parent helps at home.

Parents can offer disciplinary backing. Realistically, you are limited in what you can do when a student chooses to misbehave. The supportive feedback and corrective actions you exercise in or after class work for some students. There are other students, however, who need to know that parents will also follow through with disciplinary measures at home for misbehavior exhibited at school. When misbehavior at school means a loss of privileges at home, there is a much greater likelihood of a student's choosing to behave. By the same token, when improved behavior at school is recognized with supportive feedback at home, there is a much greater chance that the student will continue to choose appropriate behavior.

To illustrate more clearly, look at the parent involvement issue from the perspective of another group of professionals who deal with children: pediatricians. The pediatrician knows that it is her responsibility to diagnose a child's problem, prescribe treatment, and carefully explain to parents what they must do to help their child. The pediatrician then fully expects that parents will support her efforts. If a parent complains with "I work, I can't make sure he takes his medicine," or "I'm too busy to get her to her checkup," the doctor will lay it on the line: "I cannot make sure your child gets better unless you do your part."

The issues that you as a teacher deal with are every bit as immediate and important as those the pediatrician faces. Children who experience school failure have a higher probability of ending up on drugs, in jail, or on welfare. These outcomes can be as serious as most physical problems a child will encounter, and you have every right to parent support as a doctor does, for teachers and doctors are both professionals responsible for the well-being and growth of a child.

Parents are usually willing to get involved in their child's education, yet for many reasons they are often reluctant to do so. Effective teachers put in the time and effort it takes to get these parents involved. These teachers communicate to parents that they honestly care about their children's success in school and, ultimately, in life.

Effective teachers adapt their schedules to include late evening or weekend conferences in order to be accessible for all parents. Effective teachers contact parents repeatedly and at any time or place necessary to speak with even the hard-to-reach parent. Effective teachers are willing to offer support and guidance to parents who are not sure how to improve their children's academic or behavior skills. Effective teachers show respect and understanding for the parents' concerns and insights at all times, and are willing to adapt their strategies based on a parent's justified criticism. Effective teachers are willing to cooperate with parents, and do their best to listen to and incorporate the parents' insights into a student's problem rather than to impose the teacher's point of view. Effective teachers use proactive strategies to involve parents in their children's life at school before problems even arise, and to establish a positive relationship with the entire family.

Effective teachers do everything in their power to reach out to parents who may feel left out of their children's life at school.

Effective teachers demonstrate concern for the child.

A great concern of parents is that their child's teacher will not put in the time and effort necessary to ensure that their child succeeds in school. Effective teachers know this and take steps to alleviate these parental worries. Experience has shown them that when a parent believes that a teacher really cares about their child, that parent is not as likely to argue, make excuses, or question the teacher's competency. Instead, the parent will make every effort to support the teacher.

Here are some strategies that effective teachers use to demonstrate concern for their students.

From the beginning of the school year, communicate that you care about the student's success.

It is never too early to show parents you care. Many teachers begin even before the school year starts. A welcoming phone call or note home to parents of incoming students can go a long way toward demonstrating your interest in their children. In Chapters 4 and 5, we will be discussing a few strategies that will get your relationship with your students' parents off to a good start.

Establish positive communication with parents.

The key to showing genuine concern is to contact parents when the child is doing something right. When parents hear good news, it's easier for them to believe that you really do care. You will also find that once you've established positive communication with parents, they will be much more receptive when you have to call them with a problem.

Most parents report that they hear from the teacher only when there is a problem. When every communication is negative, it's easy to understand why parents avoid contact with teachers. After all, most parents would like to believe that their child is doing something right at school, at least some of the time. In

Chapter 6, we will be looking at a variety of ways to communicate with parents in positive ways.

Take every opportunity to show you care.

In every interaction with parents, all eyes are on you. Don't miss any opportunity to let parents know that you care about their child. Failure to show concern may miscommunicate to the parent a lack of caring on your part. From the start, look for occasions that will show your interest and concern. Notes home, phone calls, birthday greetings, and get-well cards not only address the occasion but also consistently demonstrate to parents that your commitment to their child is genuine. Throughout Section 2, you will find useful ideas and tips for how to incorporate proactive relationship building with your students' parents into your daily life as a teacher.

Effective teachers treat parents the way they would want to be treated.

Teachers who are most successful in getting parent support adhere to the "golden rule" of positive parent relations: Treat parents the way you would want to be treated if you had a child in school. This common-sense approach to positive parent involvement is one of the most valuable qualities you can develop.

By following the golden rule, you will gain two important advantages:

1. Through your words and actions, you will consistently demonstrate to parents that you are a concerned and caring teacher. Your underlying message at all times will be, "I understand your needs and I will be sensitive to them."

2. You will have a guideline for determining how you will approach and deal with parents in all situations. When you ask yourself, *What would I as a parent want to see happen in this situation?* the answer will usually be surprisingly clear.

For example:

■ *If I had a child in school, what specific information would I want to hear from the teacher at the beginning of the year?*

■ *How and when would I want to be approached about a problem?*

- *How would I want to be spoken to?*

- *How would I want to be listened to?*

- *Would I want to hear from the teacher when my child is doing well or only when there is a problem?*

Putting yourself in the parents' place can take the guesswork out of determining how to handle many situations. Respect for the parents will follow naturally, as will an increased ability to take their input seriously.

You will find the golden rule mentioned throughout *Parents on Your Side* because it is the guiding force behind many of the techniques and suggestions given. Keep it in mind because it applies to all the issues discussed.

Effective teachers demonstrate professionalism and confidence.

You can be the most skilled teacher in the world, but if parents don't recognize your competence, you'll have a difficult time getting their support. What can you do to demonstrate your professionalism and let parents know you have confidence in your own ability?

Involve parents.

A confident teacher welcomes the support and involvement of parents and is not intimidated by the help a parent can offer. A confident teacher views education as a team effort, and parents as part of that team.

Professionalism in dealing with parents requires that you have a plan for working with parents all year long. Parent involvement is not a twice-a-year event. It is a daily responsibility. It cannot be left to chance encounters and sporadic conversations. You need to know exactly when, how, and why you will contact parents from the first day of school to the last. You need to develop a parent involvement plan.

A parent involvement plan is your plan of action for dealing with parents throughout the year. This plan is not a strict, step-by-step prescription. A successful parent involvement plan is one that you develop to meet your specific needs and the needs of your students and their parents. In the following chapters you will find practical techniques that you can use to get and keep parent support—in all situations, at all grade levels, and with all kinds of parents. These techniques will be your guide for developing a plan of your own.

Demonstrate your confidence.

Show your confidence in every interaction with parents. Each time you meet with a parent, speak with a parent on the phone, or send a note home, you have a new opportunity to shine. Make the most of these opportunities. Stop and think a minute before you speak or write a note. Be professional, confident, and assertive. Then let your words and attitude carry that message forth.

Communicate clearly and assertively.

Assured communication—communication that says, "I know what I'm doing"— is vital to working effectively with parents. Would you hire an attorney who vacillated on how to advise you? Why should a parent be expected to support a teacher who does not appear to have confidence in her own abilities? You have to impress upon parents that you do in fact know what you're doing. You have to learn to project the attitude of self-assurance that earns respect and promotes confidence. That means learning communication skills.

In Chapter 3, we will look at some of the roadblocks that keep parents and teachers from communicating effectively.

CHAPTER 3

Recognizing Roadblocks

Despite the nationwide trend to involve parents and communities in the process of formal education, what still defines our role models of administrators, teachers, and parents are attitudes that strictly separate home from school. Administrators tend to call the shots, teachers consider themselves the experts on a student's education, and parents view school with a bias ranging from complacency to combativeness.[1]

These attitudes block the road to an open two-way communication between teacher and parent.

You as a teacher need to recognize, address, and ultimately remove two kinds of roadblocks before you can successfully cooperate with your students' parents. This chapter covers the following:

■ Teachers' roadblocks—obstacles that keep teachers from initiating communication

■ Parents' roadblocks—obstacles that keep parents from giving support

Be aware of teachers' roadblocks.

A teacher's effective attitude when working with parents is only as effective as the teacher's ability to communicate it.

■ If you find yourself doubting whether or not it is your responsibility to handle a problem situation, you may find yourself on unsure ground when you try to solve it.

■ If you feel that you've never been trained to work with parents, then you may find yourself stumbling over your own words and actions.

■ If you have negative feelings about working with parents in general, it can easily appear as a lack of confidence and competence.

Following are three types of roadblocks that often prevent teachers from asking for the help they need from parents.

Teachers' Roadblock #1: The Myth of the "Good Teacher"

"Our district wants parents happy at all costs. We are basically told to handle problems on our own. If we go to parents for help, they'll think we don't know what we're doing."

"Everyone expects us to handle problems with our students on our own. It's a clear message at this school that if you have to involve parents, the administration thinks you're not up to snuff."

The myth of the "good teacher"—the notion that competent teachers should handle all their students' problems on their own—still permeates many schools and school districts. Many administrators have fostered this myth by discouraging teachers from contacting parents when problems arise. Many parents have fostered this myth by responding in a negative manner when teachers call. The underlying assumption seems to be that teachers should handle it all by themselves, that it is not "professional" to involve parents.

Do you

■ wait until the last minute before calling a parent about a problem?

■ avoid talking to parents because you are afraid they will judge you?

■ apologize to parents when you do speak with them?

■ negate problems?

■ avoid talking with your administrator about problems you are having with students or parents?

If you answered yes to any of these questions, you probably buy into the myth of the good teacher. This is important for you to recognize. If you feel less than professional when you need to work with parents, you will present yourself to others not as a competent and confident professional but as an unsure, faltering novice.

Here's an example of how the myth of the good teacher can creep into a phone conversation between parent and teacher.

The conversation begins with an apology.

Teacher: I'm really sorry to bother you at home. I know how busy you are.

The teacher then proceeds to belittle her own abilities.

Teacher: I really just don't know what to do with Sara. She had problems again today, and I guess I don't know what else to try with her.

The teacher minimizes the severity of the problem.

Teacher: Sara hit another student today. Well, she didn't really hurt her.

The teacher continues in an ineffectual way to ask for support.

Teacher: As I said, I'm not too sure what to do at this time. I know you've got six other kids and plenty of problems of your own, but if you have the time, I'd really appreciate it if you'd have a word with Sara.

The uncertainty communicated with a weak communication style may be why teachers do not get parents on their side. Look more closely at what went on in that conversation.

First, this teacher, like many teachers, began a parent conversation by apologizing. There is no reason to apologize! Apologies are given when you feel that you have done something wrong. You are calling the parent not to bother her but to discuss what can be done to help the child. Making this call is your job and your responsibility.

Second, this teacher belittled her own professional abilities. Teachers often say things to parents such as, "I don't know what to do with him." Such statements do not exude confidence or professionalism. Instead, these statements lead parents to believe that you are incompetent and incapable of handling their child. Obviously, this can be frustrating to parents, especially those with children who have problems.

Let's return to the pediatrician analogy. Assume that your own child is ill. You take your child to the doctor, who runs some tests and calls you back the next day. She says to you,

"I'm really sorry to bother you at home. I know how busy you are. I have the tests back and I'm really not sure what is going on with your child, but I think she has some kind of bacterial infection. As I said, I know you're busy, but if you could find the time, I'd really appreciate it if you'd go to the pharmacy and get your child some penicillin. Okay?"

This is an exaggerated example, but think about it for a moment. How would you feel about this doctor? Would you ever take your child back to see her? Would you have any confidence in this doctor? Would you support this doctor? The answer is the same: no. But this is exactly the situation going on today with many teachers. They do not know what to say. They do not know how to say it. They are so tied up in the myth of the good teacher that they do not feel that they have the right to ask for parent support. This attitude is reflected in everything they say to parents. Keep the pediatrician analogy in mind as you continue to read through this book. You will find that the analogy is pertinent to many of your professional situations.

The myth of the good teacher keeps too many teachers who really are good at everything else they do from working effectively with parents.

Does this roadblock apply to you? If so, you must learn to overcome it if you are going to establish support from parents. In this book, you will learn the techniques and gain the confidence to do so.

Teacher's Roadblock #2: The Myth of the "Bad Parent"

"You can't reach parents, and if you do, all you hear is that they don't know what to do and they want you to handle the problem. Why bother trying to work with them?"

The flip side of the coin bearing the myth of the good teacher is the myth of the "bad parent." Teachers, like everyone else, may be affected by stereotypes. For example, some teachers may believe that parents from a disadvantaged socioeconomic background are less equipped to be good parents. Often parents from disadvantaged backgrounds had very little schooling themselves and thus—so the teachers think—have very little interest in their children's efforts at school. Other teachers may think that parents of different ethnic or cultural backgrounds may not share their educational values. Still others may feel that a single-parent household cannot offer the support necessary to raise an emotionally stable child.

These misconceptions are detrimental to any productive communication with parents. If teachers believe that parents are not doing their job and have no valuable insights to offer, they will most likely not try to reach out to them in order to solicit their help.

Do you

- believe that parents don't take the time or make the effort to get involved in their children's education?

- consider a student's problem proof of a parent's failure?

- contact parents to complain rather than to get their input?

- tell parents how to handle their child's problem?

- disregard a parent's point of view?

- discard a parent's concern?

If you answered yes to any of these questions, you probably are buying into the myth of the bad parent.

Not only will this attitude keep you, the teacher, from reaching out to parents, it will also keep parents from offering their help, because it is clearly not appreciated.

The truth is that all parents care. They may just not know how to show it, or they may show it in a way that you do not approve of. It is not in your or your students' best interest to underestimate parents. In fact, it is your responsibility to reach out to all parents to get them involved.

Most parents know their children better than you do and care about them greatly. If you cooperate with a parent, you'll be able to see the student in a different context, one that might show you what parents have accomplished rather than where they have failed. Practical tips and strategies for dealing with parents from different backgrounds will enable you to realize if and when your attitude toward a specific student may be informed by negative attitudes about his background. If you reach out to and cooperate with parents, you can and will move beyond your misconceptions to recognize and build upon a family's strength rather than its failures.

The myth of the bad parent may be based on experience.

Nonproductive encounters with parents can lead teachers to develop negative expectations. These negative expectations can easily lead to negative feelings about working with parents at all. When this happens, parent contact quickly breaks down, often resulting in a parent being called only as a last resort, when a problem is totally out of hand or at a crisis state.

Consider this situation: A group of middle school teachers were having academic and behavioral problems with a large number of their students. Upon examination of their grade books, it was apparent that there were students who had not completed an assignment for weeks. Other students had been given five to 10 detentions. When asked what contact they had had with parents, it became clear that not one of them had called a parent. When asked why parents had not been contacted, one teacher summed up the attitude of the others: "The parents in this area don't back us up and don't care. They want us not only to educate the children but to raise them, too!" These teachers felt that there was no value in taking the time and effort to work with their students' parents.

A teacher's negative expectations are often a direct result of having been questioned and criticized by parents. Many teachers say that the most stressful part of their job is working with angry, critical parents. When a teacher has had several unproductive conferences with hostile parents, is subjected to parents who threaten to sue or go to the school board, or is threatened with bodily harm, it is easy to understand why the teacher might become defensive or anxious.

The negativity educators sometimes feel toward parents can be a major roadblock to getting parents on your side.

Bear in mind that negative expectations are based on yesterday's experiences. Tomorrow is a new day. Begin the new day armed with a positive attitude toward parent involvement and with the skills and techniques for dealing with parents presented in *Parents on Your Side.*

Teacher's Roadblock #3:
Lack of Training in Working With Parents

"I know that I avoid dealing with parents. I'm not comfortable working with parents. I know how to work with kids; I don't know how to work with parents."

"I was trained to do one thing—to teach children. Parents were not even mentioned in my education classes."

Do you find that you avoid dealing with parents because you're just not comfortable working with them? You're not alone. Most teachers will agree that they were trained only to teach students and that parents were never even mentioned in their education classes. A study by the Harvard Family Research Project indicates that only 25 percent of the teacher education courses reviewed covered communicating with parents.[2] In the vast majority of all teacher education classes, there is, for all intents and purposes, little or no content focusing on this issue. Without training, you may find that you do not have the skills and confidence necessary to get the backing you need from parents.

Just as you need to know how to develop lesson plans for curriculum and create a discipline plan for behavior management, you also need to know how to work with parents. This requires special skills. You must learn to work with all kinds of parents, including those who question or challenge your professional competence.

To accomplish this, you must learn to listen effectively and respond accordingly—because a teacher, just like any business manager, needs to receive training in effective communication skills. *Parents on Your Side* will give you practical tips that will help you to view your students and their parents as your clients, and yourself as a customer-relations officer. We will teach you how to roll out the welcome mat and reach out to even the most reluctant parent.

Be aware of parents' roadblocks.

The roadblocks aren't all yours. Parents have roadblocks of their own that keep them from giving support. Learn to listen. Pinpointing the type of roadblock a parent might be focused on will enable you to use specific techniques to move the parent past the roadblock and get the support you need.

We have identified four parent roadblocks that typically keep parents from backing you. As you consider each one, keep in mind that by recognizing the roadblock, your response can direct the ensuing conversation to a productive conclusion.

Parents' Roadblock #1: Parents Are Overwhelmed

> "Ever since my divorce, my life has fallen apart. Sometimes I just don't feel like I can make it on my own raising a family. I know I should discipline my sons to behave at school, but really, I'd just rather the teacher handle it, because I can't cope."

When you hear a parent make comments like these, you need to know that you're dealing with a parent who is overwhelmed, that this parent is coping with a stressful situation in his life. Armed with this information, you can gear your response to moving the parent past this roadblock and avoid getting bogged down in a conversation that accomplishes nothing.

The term *at-risk student* is very popular today. We could coin another term: *at-risk parent*. These are parents who are at risk of being overwhelmed by the stress in their lives. They do not feel that they have the time or energy to support their children's education to the degree necessary to ensure their children's success.

You will find at-risk parents in all kinds of households. While it's true that many at-risk parents are part of the growing population of single parents struggling to raise and support a family on their own, it's also true that at-risk parents can be found in the most affluent two-parent homes. The point is, there can be many reasons why parents are overwhelmed with their lives: poverty, divorce, illness, or job stress. These parents may feel that school is the last thing they have the time or energy to deal with. Overwhelmed parents are a very real roadblock to getting the support you need as you learn to actively listen to what a parent is saying and react appropriately. Listen for words or phrases that will cue you to a parent's state of mind.

Here's an example of a conversation with an overwhelmed parent.

The teacher calls a parent regarding a homework problem. She introduces herself and begins discussing the problem with the parent. Before she gets very far, the parent interjects the following comments:

Parent: I hear what you're saying, but I come home so tired at night that the last thing in the world I can do is battle with my child over homework. I know he should do it, and I know I'm the one who should be making sure he does it. But I'm just too tired to deal with it.

Here are two ways a teacher could respond.

Teacher A: Mrs. Jones, Eddie has to turn in all of his homework assignments or he's going to fail this class. That's all there is to it. I don't want that to happen and, I'm sure, neither do you.

Teacher B: I hear how difficult it is for you now. I also hear you saying that you really are concerned about how your son does in school. Mrs. Jones, we both want success for him. I'm here to work with you to see that it happens. I'm going to give you some suggestions that will help you check on his homework progress each night easily and quickly.

The results:

- Teacher A failed to notice the parent's roadblock and consequently will probably end up without the support she needs to solve the problem.

- Teacher B has recognized that she is dealing with an overwhelmed parent. She knows that if she doesn't help move the parent past this roadblock, she won't get the support she needs. This teacher listened and heard. She recognized that the parent was not uncaring or hostile, but overwhelmed. She therefore adjusted her response to lead the conversation in a direction that would not cause the parent anxiety and add to her burden. Chances are good that this teacher will get the support she needs from this parent. And that means the student will get the help he needs.

Parents' Roadblock #2: Parents Want to Help but Don't Know How

> "I tell her to study. I tell her to do her homework. She says she will and then she just doesn't do it. I have no idea how to get through to this kid."

This is a parent who cares but doesn't know what to do. Each year you will encounter parents who do not have the strength or the skills needed to motivate their children to perform academically or behave appropriately in school or at home. And if parents cannot get their children to behave at home, it's not likely that they will be able to give you the support you need to ensure that their children behave in school. These are parents who need and often will accept your help. They want their children to succeed as much as you do. It is your responsibility to recognize this roadblock and get help to them.

Learn to recognize this roadblock because very often these are the parents who, with guidance and support, will be eager to become actively involved in their child's education.

Here's an example of a conversation with a parent who doesn't know how to help.

A teacher is meeting with a parent about a behavior problem. As the teacher begins to discuss the problem, the parent responds:

Parent: Believe me, I'd do something if I could. I know the way John behaves at school is wrong; he acts the same at home. I just don't have any idea what to do to help him stop. And what difference would it make anyway? He doesn't listen to a thing I say.

Here are two possible responses.

Teacher A: Well, John needs to behave at school. I can't have him disrupting my class.

Teacher B: I hear you saying that you really want to help John learn to behave at school. And I know it's not always easy to know how to do it. If you'd like, we can work together to come up with some solutions. I've worked with lots of kids just like John. I can promise you that if we put our heads together, we will come up with some solutions that will get John back on track.

The results:

■ Teacher A has pushed the problem, not the solution, onto the parent. If he had listened more effectively, he would have heard that the parent is really at a loss for what to do.

■ Teacher B realized that she was speaking with a parent who was willing to help but just didn't have any idea what to do. Knowing she had to move the parent past this roadblock, she responded by offering further suggestions for what the parent could do to remedy the problem. Through her words, this teacher let the parent know that she was concerned enough about the student to take the time to help solve the problem.

Parents' Roadblock #3: Parents' Negative Feelings About School

"I hated school. I never even graduated. The teachers were always on my case and now they're on my son's case."

Each year you will encounter parents who themselves had negative school experiences. Often when a parent did not perform well academically, was constantly in trouble, or dropped out of school, the parent harbors negative feelings about school in general and teachers in particular. These parents often do not trust teachers and may feel that teachers do not have their children's best interests at heart. Since these parents had negative experiences in school, they tend to avoid involvement in school activities. It is often difficult to get them to come to Back-to-School Night, parent conferences, school performances, and other events.

Finally, these parents may actually expect their children to have academic or behavioral problems in school just like they did. Their own experiences may lead them to believe that this is just how children behave in school. Thus, these parents tend to feel that there is no reason to get involved in solving their child's problems because there is nothing that really can be done about them.

Because a parent's negative attitude can easily be transferred to the child, it is important to recognize this roadblock and take steps to get these parents positively involved.

Here's an example of a conversation with a parent who has negative feelings about school.

The teacher calls a parent to discuss an academic problem. As soon as the teacher begins to speak, the parent goes on the offensive.

Parent: You teachers today don't like kids any more than my teachers did. All you ever do is call me and tell me how bad my kids are.

Here are two possible responses.

Teacher A: Mr. Smith, I'm calling because your son isn't performing as he should in my class.

Teacher B: Mr. Smith, I'm much more interested in calling you to let you know how terrific your son is. He has great potential. That's why it's so important that we both work together to solve this problem. Your son can be doing a lot better in class. I want to see that happen. I care about your son's success, and I know you do, too.

The results:

- Teacher A ignored the parent's roadblock and continued to address her original agenda. Ignoring the parent's anger won't defuse it. The conversation will probably lead to a dead end. The parent will still be hostile and the teacher will still not have support.

- Teacher B determined that he was speaking with a parent who had strong negative feelings about teachers and school in general. He knew that this parent would never listen to anything until this roadblock was removed. The teacher let this parent know that he in fact was dealing with a teacher who does care.

Parents' Roadblock #4:
Parents' Negative View of Teacher Competence

"Schools have gone downhill. I know it. Everyone in the neighborhood knows it. I'm not going to stand by and let my child's teacher ruin his school experience."

From time to time, you will encounter parents who simply do not respect your professional expertise. There are several reasons why this is so. First, hardly a week goes by that there isn't media attention focusing on the "dismal" state of the American educational system, focusing in particular on the poor performance of students. In many instances, the blame is placed on the teachers. Parents cannot help but absorb this constant negativity regarding the educational system.

Second, there are more parents today with a higher level of educational sophistication than ever before. Many of these parents have their own theories of how their child should be educated and will not hesitate to state these opinions, valid or invalid, to the teacher.

Third, there are, unfortunately, still some teachers who are not competent enough to meet the needs of students. The inability of the educational system to remove these teachers has added tremendous fuel to the fire of parental discontent. All it takes is one incompetent teacher in a building to stir the wrath of parents. When these teachers are not removed, the frustration level of parents and colleagues increases and an entire school can be labeled inadequate.

Keep in mind that negative views of a teacher's competence can come across in many forms, from outright hostility to subtle questioning. To defuse this negativity, you need to really listen to what a parent is saying, not just react defensively or in anger.

Here is an example of a conversation with a parent who has negative feelings about school.

The parent calls the teacher about a low grade her daughter has earned.

Parent: My child is special and I want a teacher who can meet her special needs. I will not sit by and settle for anything less.

Here are two possible responses.

Teacher A: I'm doing the best I can with her.

Teacher B: You're right to want the best for your child. That's why I want to work with you to see that she is successful in my class.

The results:

■ Teacher A let the parent get to her. She was probably hurt and became defensive. Her weak response will only make the parent angrier and feel more justified about her assumptions. The teacher's response certainly will not increase the parent's confidence in her.

■ Teacher B knows she is listening to a parent who has a negative attitude regarding teacher competence. And she knows that reactionary responses will get her nowhere. She therefore accepts the parent's sense of urgency and demonstrates strength, assurance, and confidence in her own ability.

Be sensitive to obstacles to effective communication.

Recognizing your own roadblocks is the first step toward an attitude that accepts parent involvement as both your right and your duty as a teacher. By listening for parents' roadblocks and responding accordingly, you can open communication and work together to solve problems. Once you recognize the roadblocks that stand in the way of parent involvement, you can start taking steps to remedy it.

It's a matter of sensitivity—of taking the time to think about what you really expect from a parent and what a parent really expects from you. You can't do your best for your students without the support of their parents. And parents can't give that support if they are focused on anger, confusion, or their own negative expectations. Moving every conversation with parents forward to a productive conclusion is the way to get parents on your side. You must always ask for and listen to the parent's point of view in order to demonstrate that you care about the student and his home. Hearing what is said, and adjusting your responses accordingly, is the foundation of effective communication.

References

[1] Cavarretta, J. (1998, May). Parents are a school's best friend. *Educational Leadership,* *55*(8), 12–15.

[2] Lynn, L. (1997, September/October). Teaching teachers to work with families. *Harvard Education Letter.* [Online]. Available: http://www.edletter.org/past/issues/1997-so/teaching.shtml.

How to Work With Parents to Establish Positive Relationships

Section 2 of *Parents on Your Side* will give you step-by-step suggestions for how to establish a positive relationship with parents from the start. Proactive parent involvement measures are techniques and strategies a teacher employs on a regular basis with all parents *before* a problem arises in order to establish a positive relationship.

Chapter 4: Meeting First-Day Objectives
This chapter offers suggestions to reach out to parents on or before the first day of school. Contacting parents to introduce yourself will get your relationship off to a good start.

Chapter 5: Making the Most of Back-to-School Night
These suggestions will turn Back-to-School Night into a success that will last all year long.

Chapter 6: Establishing Positive Communication with Parents
Positive communication cannot stop at the beginning of the year. This chapter presents a few efficient and effective strategies to keep in touch with the parents of all your students.

Chapter 7: Involving Parents in the Homework Process
This chapter turns homework into a successful activity between parents and students, and makes sure that parents stay involved in their children's daily lives at school.

Chapter 8: Conducting Regularly Scheduled Parent Conferences

This chapter focuses on parent conferences, which are the most effective and efficient way to communicate with parents.

Chapter 9: Demonstrating Sensitivity and Awareness

Awareness and sensitivity, the two most important guidelines offered in this chapter, are the basis and prerequisite for any and all communication techniques discussed throughout this book.

Consistent and continued positive communication with parents throughout the year will help you establish a relationship with parents that you can build upon should problems arise.

Meeting First-Day Objectives

Start working as soon as possible to get the parent support you need. It's up to you to make the first move. From the very beginning, you must clearly communicate that parental involvement and support is necessary and valued. Don't wait until a problem comes up. Don't wait for parents to come to you. Reach out to them right away. Parent contact needs to begin before the first day of school.

The first actions you take will quickly help to establish your reputation with parents as an effective professional who not only cares about the welfare of their children but who has the confidence and skills to take charge. Set immediate objectives for yourself and take the actions that will achieve them. The purpose of meeting these objectives is to break down potential communication barriers, get past existing roadblocks, and set the stage for productive communication and cooperation all year long.

This chapter covers three objectives for you to meet on or before the first day of school:

- Send a "before school starts" greeting to all parents and incoming students.

- Open up verbal communication with parents of potential problem students.

- Communicate your expectations to parents.

Send a "before school starts" greeting to parents and students.

Before the beginning of the school year, you are probably unknown to most of your students' parents, and perhaps to the students themselves. Introduce yourself by saying a friendly hello. Take time during vacation—before school starts— to drop a line to incoming students and their parents. You don't need to say much, just let them know that you're enthusiastic about the upcoming year. Here are two examples.

Sample "Before School Starts" Greetings

> Dear Mr. and Mrs. Rosas:
>
> Just a quick note to let you know I'm looking forward to working with Melina this year. It will be a pleasure to get to know both of you. Please feel free to drop by the classroom on the first day of school, September 10. I'd like to say hello!
>
> Sincerely,
>
> Ms. Warner

> Dear Melina:
>
> I just received my roster and found out you'll be in my algebra class. I'm looking forward to a terrific year and I hope you are, too. Enjoy the rest of your vacation. I'll see you September 10.
>
> Sincerely,
>
> Mr. Ramos

These brief notes are a preview of the many positive communications parents and students will be receiving from you throughout the year.

Open up verbal communication with parents of potential problem students.

Have you been assigned students who have a history of problems in school? Don't just complain about it in the teachers' room. Do something positive about it. Take some proactive steps to get the parents of these students on your side now, before school and the problems begin, by calling the parents. The goal of your conversation is to establish positive communication and to reassure parents that you care about their child. You also want to exhibit professionalism and confidence in your ability to work with their child.

Remember that parents of difficult students are probably used to hearing from school only when there is a problem. Here's your chance to make a difference and show them that you are a caring and supportive teacher. You are going to turn this situation around and contact them with good news. You'll let them know you are confident that you can all work together to make this a successful year for their child.

Plan what you will say.

Before making the call, write down what you want to cover, and keep your notes in front of you as you speak. This preparation will be well worth it. If you deal effectively with this first phone call, you will probably have far greater support from this parent throughout the year.

Plan to address each of the following points:

1. **Begin with a statement of support.**
   The first words you speak will set the tone for the entire conversation. Be sensitive to the parent's feelings. Keep in mind that the last thing she wants to hear are problems concerning her child, before the school year has even begun. You have to let this parent know immediately that you are calling because you care about her child and because you sincerely want to make the new year a success.

   "Mrs. Hirsch, this is Mrs. Williams. I'm going to be Bobby's fifth grade teacher. I wanted to speak to you before the school year began because I want to make sure that this year is successful for your child."

2. **Get parental input concerning the problems of last year.**
   Demonstrate your interest in the parent's point of view. Let the parent know that you genuinely care how she feels about what happened the previous year. This is the time to listen for roadblocks. Is the parent overwhelmed? Angry? Unable to deal with the child's problems? Gear your response to what the parent says to you.

   "I would like to know how you see Bobby's experience at school last year."

3. **Find out what the parent feels is necessary to make this year more successful.**

Listen to the parent's suggestions. She may be able to offer valuable insights that will help you get off to a better start with the student. The information may give you an advantage in dealing with the student from the first day.

"I'd like to know what you think we need to do to make sure Bobby has a good year this year."

4. **Explain that parent support is critical.**

Let the parent know how important her support is.

"I believe that you can help me with Bobby. I will be in touch with you throughout the year because your support is vital. You are the most important person in Bobby's life and he must know that we are working together to help him."

5. **Express your confidence.**

Put yourself in this parent's position. Another school year is starting. If it's anything like the last, it may be a continual round of negative feedback from school. Give the parent something to be optimistic about. The confidence you project will encourage the parent to give the support you need.

"I have complete confidence that by working together we will help Bobby to have a good year. I want to assure you that I've worked with all kinds of students, and I am certain I can make this year a great one for your son."

Sample Phone Conversations

Here's a sample elementary level conversation.

Parent: Hello.

Teacher: Mrs. Gowdy?

Parent: Yes.

Teacher: (Introduce yourself) This is Mrs. Tomaselli. I'll be Ted's teacher next year.

Parent: Oh, hello.

Teacher: (State reason for call) The reason I'm calling is that I want to make sure that this year is successful for Ted.

Parent: I'm glad to hear that. Last year wasn't very good for Ted at all.

Teacher: *(Get parental input)* Really? Why is that?

Parent: Oh, I don't know. The teacher and Ted didn't get along. She was very negative. They had what I guess you would call a personality conflict. I felt that she didn't know how to handle him. She would call me and expect me to do her job. You know, she's the teacher and she should handle some of those things. I sure didn't know what to do.

Teacher: I can see that last year was very frustrating for you. *(Get parental suggestion for solution)* I'd really like to hear any suggestions you might have that could help Ted have a better year this year.

Parent: My son needs a lot of attention. He's had a tough couple of years. Ever since my husband and I got divorced, Ted just doesn't seem to care about school. So far no teacher has given him the attention and support he needs.

Teacher: I understand what you're saying, and let me assure you that I will do everything I can to make it a positive, supportive year for him. In fact, I've got an idea of something we can do right at the start of the year. Every day, I have a special monitor in class, and I think it would be great if for the first few days of school Ted could be my special monitor. That will enable me to give him a lot of personal attention and positive support. I can make sure the first few days this year are really positive for him.

Parent: That may help. It's more than the teacher did last year.

Teacher: *(Express need for parental support)* I know that if we work together we can ensure success for Ted.

Parent: What do you mean by "working together"? I don't have much time. You know I work full time and have two other children.

Teacher: I understand. What I'm suggesting won't take a lot of time. But it'll make a great difference. You know, you are the most important person in Ted's life, and Ted must know we're working together to help him.

Parent: I haven't had much success with him in the past.

Teacher:	I know how frustrating it can be with children, but let me assure you that I've worked with many students like Ted. And I've worked with many of their parents and have had great success. I am going to make it a point to see that Ted has a super year. I want Ted to like school and I want him to be a success.
Parent:	You sound like you mean it.
Teacher:	I do. I mean what I say.
Parent:	I really appreciate your taking the time to call. No teacher has ever done this before.
Teacher:	It's my pleasure. I will be in touch with you throughout the year and I want you to stay in touch with me. *(Speak to child)* Before I say good-bye, I think it would help if I could speak to Ted for a few minutes to introduce myself to him and share my feelings about this year.

Here's a sample secondary level conversation.

Parent:	Hello.
Teacher:	Mrs. Greenfield?
Parent:	Yes.
Teacher:	This is Mr. Schwartz. I'll be Gail's social studies teacher next year. *(State reason for call)* The reason I'm calling is that I noticed that Gail had a lot of trouble with social studies last year. *(Get parental input)* I'd like to find out why she had these problems and what we can do to make sure they don't occur this year.
Parent:	Well, I think I can tell you what the problem was. I think she had a poor attitude toward school.
Teacher:	I hear what you're saying. Can you tell me specifically what happened last year with her schoolwork?
Parent:	Sometimes she told me she didn't have any homework when, actually, she did. And the few times she did do it, she would race through it just to finish it. She wouldn't care whether she did a good job. She'd do it while she was on the phone with the stereo blasting or the TV on.

Teacher:	It sounds like you had a few difficulties. *(Get parental suggestion for solution)* Do you have any suggestions about what I can do to help the situation this year?
Parent:	I really don't know. To be honest, she probably needs a new group of friends. The kids she hangs out with are no good.
Teacher:	I can't get her new friends, but I think maybe there are some things I can do as her teacher to help.
Parent:	Well, she says she doesn't believe that teachers really care. Teachers could care less if she comes to class, or if she does or doesn't do her work. It never matters.
Teacher:	Well, I'm a teacher who does care. I'll make sure she knows that.
Parent:	I don't know. She hasn't liked teachers and she hasn't liked school since the seventh grade. She's really been lost. Just lost.
Teacher:	I think lots of kids get lost today in schools the size of ours. I don't want her to get lost. That's why I'm calling. I want to work with her to make sure she is involved and does her class work and her homework.
Parent:	She needs a lot of help. She has no idea how to study.
Teacher:	I can help her there. I can teach her some very simple, basic study skills that will help her to be more successful. *(Express need for parental support)* I will do my part, but I'm going to need your help if we are going to turn things around for Gail.
Parent:	But she doesn't listen to me. I'm not even usually home when she does her homework. I'm at work, and I don't know what I can do from there.
Teacher:	I don't want you to worry. I've worked with many students like your daughter. I've also worked with many parents in your position, and let me assure you, we can help her. Throughout the year I'll give you guidelines and techniques that will help Gail study more successfully. I'll follow through at school, and you can follow through at home. How does that sound?
Parent:	I really appreciate your attitude. But I still don't know if it will do any good.

Teacher: I know it will. We will work together. We will help your daughter. She is going to succeed in my class. With me doing my part and you doing your part, it will work. You can count on me. I will be behind you 100 percent.

Communicate your expectations to parents.

If they are to be actively involved, parents need some basic information right at the beginning of the school year. First, they need to know a little bit about you. After all, you are going to be an influential person in your students' lives. It's important that parents have an opportunity to know something more about you than your name and room number.

Second, parents of both elementary and secondary students need to know the teacher's classroom rules and standards. Think a minute about the parent contacts you have had in the past. What precipitated many of these contacts? Chances are it was either a behavior problem or a homework problem. These are, after all, the day-to-day problems that you deal with most often. It is extremely important that you communicate to parents your standards and policies for both areas. You can't ask parents to back up your rules if they don't know them. Before school begins, you should formulate both a classroom discipline plan and a homework policy.

Send home the following on the first day of school:

- A letter of introduction
- A copy of your discipline plan
- A copy of your homework policy

Suggestions follow for generating these items.

Send home a letter of introduction.

Give parents an opportunity to know something about you and your plans for the upcoming year.

- Keep your letter brief; no more than one page.
- The tone of your letter should be upbeat and enthusiastic.

- Take this opportunity to tell parents that you need their support—that the education of their children is a team effort.

- Above all, end the letter with a statement expressing your confidence in the success you expect for all of your students this year.

Sample Letter of Introduction to Parents

Dear Parents,

My name is Mr. Camacho, and I will be your child's fifth grade teacher this year. I'm looking forward to an exciting, productive year working with you and your child.

Throughout my years of teaching, I have become committed to the importance of parent involvement in a student's education. I firmly believe that your child receives the best education possible when you and I work as a team.

Enclosed with this letter are copies of my classroom discipline plan and my homework policy. Please read both of these carefully. They explain many of my expectations for your child in this class. I need your support of these expectations, and I need you to let your child know also that you support these classroom rules and standards.

I will be keeping in close touch with you all year long. Please do the same with me. I welcome your calls and messages. Any time you have something you'd like to discuss with me, please call the school office at 555-2222. I will return your call as quickly as possible.

I look forward to meeting you at Back-to-School Night on September 24. It's going to be an exciting evening that I know you won't want to miss.

Sincerely,

Mr. Camacho

Formulate your classroom discipline plan.

A classroom discipline plan[1] determines your policies regarding behavior management. It provides a system of guidelines that clarify the behaviors you expect from your students. It also establishes what they can expect from you in return if they follow your guidelines, and if they don't. Such a clearly defined policy is the prerequisite for a structured and supportive classroom environment in which all students are treated consistently with fairness. A discipline plan ensures your students' emotional and physical safety and allows you to focus on teaching, and your students on learning.

These guidelines for formulating a discipline plan incorporate the strategies for behavior management developed in our book *Assertive Discipline*. Obviously, there are other behavior management techniques upon which a classroom discipline plan may be based. While *Assertive Discipline* provides effective techniques for classroom management, use the strategies that best suit your teaching style. It is important that you develop some plan that clarifies your policy regarding behavior management. You, your students, and their parents have a need and the right to know which behaviors you expect, and the supportive and corrective measures you will take to encourage and enforce these behaviors.

In defining such a plan, it is important that you don't just copy the suggestions offered here but that you use your own professional judgment to determine which classroom management strategies best fit your situation.

Whichever techniques you choose, a discipline plan is an integral part of any teacher's parent involvement plan. It lets parents know exactly how their children are to behave, what will happen when they do behave, and what will happen when they don't.

A classroom discipline plan should address at least the following three areas:

1. Rules students must follow at all times

2. Corrective actions students will receive for not following the rules

3. Supportive feedback students will receive for following the rules

Having well-defined rules and predetermined corrective actions from the very beginning will assist you in your teaching efforts and give you a basis for effectively communicating with parents. Based on your discipline plan, you will be able to

■   judge student behavior fairly;

Sample Discipline Plan Letter

Classroom Discipline Plan
Room 5   Mr. Bronson

Dear Parent(s):

These are the rules of my classroom. These rules will be in effect at all times:

- ➤ Follow directions.
- ➤ Keep hands, feet, and objects to yourself.
- ➤ No teasing or name calling is allowed.
- ➤ Do not leave the room without permission.

If a student chooses to break a rule, the following corrective actions will be imposed:

First time a student breaks a rule:	Reminder
Second time:	Five minutes away from group
Third time:	Ten minutes away from group
Fourth time:	Teacher calls parents with student
Fifth time:	Send to principal

Severe misbehavior, such as fighting or verbal abuse, will result in the immediate imposition of the Severe Clause: Send to principal.

Students who behave appropriately will be supported with verbal reinforcement, positive notes sent home, small rewards, class parties, and other special privileges.

I have already discussed this plan with your child, but I would appreciate it if you would review it together, then sign and return the form below.

Thank you for your support.

Sincerely,

Mr. Bronson

- -

I have read the discipline plan and have discussed it with my child.

Parent's signature _____

Student's signature _____

Date _____

■ discuss behavior problems more confidently with parents, because you can accurately describe to a parent

➤ the rule(s) that the student has broken;

➤ the corrective actions following the student's misbehavior;

➤ the supportive feedback following the student's compliance with your rules.

Send your discipline plan home.

Once you've defined your classroom discipline plan, it is important that you allow parents to take a look at it so that they may know how their children will be dealt with at school in case of discipline problems. Include a sign-off portion that is to be returned to you, indicating that the parent has read the discipline plan. (See page 45.)

Determine your homework policy.

Because homework provides a day-to-day connection between home and school, it is one of the best opportunities you have for positive interaction with parents. Homework has the potential to be a powerful part of your parent involvement program. Too often, however, homework becomes a bone of contention between parents, students, and teachers. Any positive interaction that might result from it is lost in a sea of misinformation and unfulfilled expectations.

If you want parents to give the support you need regarding homework, it is important that your homework standards are clearly spelled out. As much as you need to develop a discipline plan to communicate your disciplinary standards, you need to develop a homework policy to clearly communicate your homework standards. A homework policy clearly states your expectations for everyone involved in the homework process: student, teacher, and parents.

Elements of a Homework Policy
A homework policy should

1. explain why homework is assigned;

2. explain the types of homework you will assign;

3. inform parents of the amount and frequency of homework;

4. provide guidelines for when and how students are to complete homework;

5. state that you will keep a record of assignments completed and not completed;

6. explain how homework will affect students' grades;

7. inform parents and students of test schedules;

8. let parents know how you will positively reinforce students who complete homework;

9. explain what you will do when students do not complete homework (effect on grades, etc.);

10. clarify what is expected of the parent.

Look more closely at each of these elements of a homework policy.

1. **Explain why homework is assigned.**
   You can't assume that parents understand why homework is given or how important it is. Therefore, you must explain the benefits of homework. For instance, your rationale could include that homework is important because

   - it reinforces skills and material learned in class;

   - it prepares students for upcoming class topics;

   - it teaches students to work independently;

   - it aids in evaluating student progress;

   - it teaches students to assume responsibility for their own work;

   - it teaches students organizational and time-management skills.

2. **Explain the types of homework you will assign.**
   It is important that both parents and students know that you are doing your part to ensure that students have the ability to do the homework you assign. Your policy should state that the homework you assign requires only those skills students have already learned in class.

3. **Inform parents of the amount and frequency of homework.**
   If parents are to back up your homework program, they must know when to expect assignments. Research has shown that regular homework assignments

are more effective than homework assigned inconsistently. It is important, therefore, for you to include in your homework policy

- the days of the week on which you will assign homework;

- the amount of time it should take students to complete homework.

The amount of homework you assign will depend on your community, your district, your principal, your class, and even the individual student.

4. Provide guidelines for when and how students are to complete homework. For students to meet your expectations about completing homework, you must clearly explain how you expect them to do their assignments. Typical expectations include:

- All assignments will be completed.

- Students will do homework on their own and to the best of their ability.

- Students will turn in work that is neatly done.

- Students will turn in homework on time.

- Students are responsible for making up homework assignments missed due to absence.

5. State that you will keep a record of assignments completed and not completed.
Your policy should state that you will keep a daily record of all homework assignments completed and not completed. The fact that you will check all homework is enough to motivate many students to do their homework. Also, this type of record keeping says something to both students and parents about the value you place on each and every assignment.

6. Explain how homework will affect students' grades.
Students and parents alike need to know if homework will be graded separately or as a percentage of another grade. Many schools list homework as a separate item on report cards. Others consider homework as part of a subject grade. The system you use should be stated in your homework policy.

7. Inform parents and students of test schedules.
It is important that parents and students (especially in upper grades) know when tests will be scheduled and how they will be evaluated. The follow-

ing is an example of a homework policy statement regarding tests for a math class.

"Tests will be given periodically, usually on a Wednesday or a Friday. Adequate notice will be given for all tests. To prepare for tests, go over notes and corrected homework assignments. Any test that receives a D or an F must be returned within two days signed by a parent."

8. **Let parents know how you will positively reinforce students who complete homework.**
   Research has shown that positive reinforcement is useful in motivating students to do homework. Your policy, therefore, should include

   - supportive feedback for individual students—praise, awards, and notes home to the parents;

   - rewards that can be earned by the entire class.

9. **Explain what you will do when students do not complete homework.**
   It is important that students and parents clearly understand the corrective actions that will be imposed for not doing homework. Examples of actions that can be taken include the following:

   - Have parents sign completed homework every night.

   - Have elementary students miss recess to complete homework.

   - Have secondary students eat lunch while completing homework.

   - Have students complete homework after school.

   - Lower students' grades.

   Whatever corrective actions you choose must be clearly spelled out in your homework policy.
       Let parents know that homework missed for legitimate reasons must be explained in a signed note from them.

10. **Clarify what is expected of the parent.**
    Since you do not follow the homework and the students home, it is up to parents to see that homework is completed. Your homework policy needs to cover the specific type of support you expect from parents. You should expect parents to

- establish homework as a top priority for their children;

- make sure that their children do homework in a quiet environment;

- establish a daily homework time;

- provide supportive feedback when homework is completed;

- not allow children a way out of doing homework;

- contact you if children have problems with homework.

Send your homework policy home.

Parents need to receive your homework policy before the first homework assignments are given. Take a look at the sample homework policy letters to parents on pages 52 to 55. Notice that each of the elements previously listed is included in the letters.

It's worth the effort.

Take a moment to look back at the first-day goals in terms of moving parents past their roadblocks. How do you think parents will react to receiving these notes, letters, and phone calls?

- An overwhelmed parent will be relieved and pleased that his child has a teacher who is taking charge and who obviously cares about the student. This parent will appreciate the confidence the teacher has shown in taking a proactive stance.

- A parent who wants to help but doesn't know how to do so will feel that the ice has been broken. With the introduction that has been made, she will feel much more comfortable approaching you for help.

- Finally, a parent who has negative feelings toward school in general or teachers in particular will most likely have been nudged just a little bit closer to a more positive attitude toward both.

You are setting the stage for a full year of positive parent involvement. By meeting each of the objectives above, you demonstrate to parents that you are committed to your parent involvement program. This in turn will communicate that you are committed to their children's success. Certainly, this will be greatly appreciated.

Putting in time and energy early will save you even greater effort in the future. These are preventive actions that will put your parent involvement program on the right track from the start.

Sample Homework Policy for a Fourth Grade Class

Room 6 Homework Policy

To the family of _____

Why I assign homework:

I believe homework is important because it is a valuable aid in help-ing students make the most of their experience in school. I give home-work because it is useful in reinforcing what has been learned in class, prepares students for upcoming lessons, teaches responsibility, and helps students develop positive study habits.

When homework will be assigned:

Homework will be assigned Monday through Thursday nights. Assign-ments should take students no more than one hour to complete each night, not including studying for tests and working on projects. Spelling tests will be given each Friday. I will give students at least one week's notice to study for all tests, and one written report will be assigned each grading period.

Student's homework responsibilities:

I expect students to do their best job on their homework. I expect homework to be neat, not sloppy. I expect students to do the work on their own and ask for help only after they have given it their best effort. I expect that all assignments will be turned in on time.

Teacher's homework responsibilities:

I will check all homework. Because I strongly believe in the value sup-portive feedback plays in motivating children to develop good study habits, I will recognize students when they do their homework and offer incentives.

Parent's homework responsibilities:

Parents are the key to making homework a positive experience for their children. Therefore, I ask that parents make homework a top priority, provide necessary supplies and a quiet homework environment, set a daily homework time, provide praise and support, not let children avoid doing homework, and contact me if they notice a problem.

If students do not complete homework:

If students choose not to do their homework, I will ask that parents begin checking and signing completed homework each night. If students choose to make up homework the next day, their homework will be accepted but they will receive a one-grade reduction on that assignment. If they choose not to make up missed assignments, students will receive a grade of F for the assignment missed.

If there is a legitimate reason why a student is not able to finish homework, please send a note to me on the day the homework is due stating the reason it was not completed. The note must be signed by the parent.

Please read and discuss this homework policy with your child. Then sign the bottom portion of this letter and return it to school.

Mrs. Kerns

- -

I have read this homework policy and have discussed it with my child.

Parent's signature _____

Student's signature _____

Date _____

Sample Homework Policy for a Ninth Grade Social Studies Class

Homework Policy
Mr. Jaworski   9th Grade Social Studies

To the family of _____

Why I assign homework:

I believe that homework is a valuable aid in helping students make the most of their experience in school. I give homework because it reinforces what has been taught in class, prepares students for upcoming lessons, and helps students develop self-discipline, responsibility, and organizational skills.

When homework will be assigned:

Homework will be assigned Monday, Tuesday, and Thursday nights, and should take students no more than one hour to complete (not including long-range projects and studying for tests).

Tests:

Tests will be given periodically, usually on a Wednesday or a Friday. Adequate notice will be given for all tests. Any test that receives a D or an F must be returned within two days, signed by a parent. Students will have at least two weeks' notice to study for tests, and one written report will be assigned each grading period.

Student's homework responsibilities:

➤ All assignments will be completed and turned in on time.
➤ Students are responsible for making up homework missed due to absence.
➤ Students will turn in work that is neatly done.

If students choose not to do their homework, the following corrective actions may occur:

➤ Parents will be asked to sign completed homework each night.
➤ Students may be required to complete homework during lunch or after school.

If there is a legitimate reason why a student is unable to finish homework, please send a note on the day the homework is due stating the reason it was not completed. The note must be signed by the parent.

Parent's homework responsibilities:

Parents are the key to making homework a positive experience for their children. Therefore, I ask that you make homework a top priority, provide necessary supplies and a quiet homework environment, provide praise and support, and contact me if you notice a problem.

Teacher's homework responsibilities:

I will check all homework and keep a record of assignments completed and not completed. Because I strongly believe in the value supportive feedback plays in motivating students to develop good study habits, I will recognize students with a variety of incentives when they do their homework.

I am looking forward to enjoying an exciting, productive year at school. Please do not hesitate to call me if you have any questions regarding this homework policy or any other matter.

Please read and discuss this homework policy with your child. Then sign the bottom portion of this letter and return it to school.

Sincerely,

Mr. Jaworski

- -

I have read this homework policy and have discussed it with my child.

Parent's signature _____

Student's signature _____

Date _____

Meeting First-Day Objectives
REMINDERS

DO

➤ Initiate parent contact before the first day of school.

➤ Formulate a classroom discipline plan before school starts.

➤ Write your homework policy before school starts.

➤ Send parents a letter stating that you need their support and that the education of their children is a team effort.

➤ Contact parents of potential problem students to let them know you are committed to their children's success in school this year.

➤ Send your discipline plan and homework policy home as soon as school begins. Ask parents to read and sign both documents.

➤ Carefully explain your discipline plan and homework policy to students on the first day of school.

➤ Feel confident in your ability to have a successful year!

DON'T

➤ Don't avoid contacting, by phone or by letter, non–English-speaking parents. Find a translator to help you and reach out to these parents. Please refer to Chapter 9 for further discussion of communicating with parents from different cultural or linguistic backgrounds.

➤ Don't wait for parents to come to you. Reach out to them first—before school starts.

Meeting First-Day Objectives
CHECKLIST

Refer to this checklist when you start your first-day objectives.

Have you:

___ sent welcome notes to parents and students before school begins?

___ sent home a letter of introduction?

___ contacted parents of problem students before school begins?

___ sent home a copy of your classroom discipline plan?

___ sent home a copy of your homework policy?

Reference

[1] Canter, L., & Canter, M. (2001). *Assertive discipline: Positive behavior management for today's classroom*. Los Angeles: Canter & Associates.

Making the Most of Back-to-School Night

Back-to-School Night can be one of the most important events of the school year for both elementary and secondary teachers. It's your opportunity to meet parents, explain your policies and programs in detail, answer any questions about your class, and, most important, assure parents of your commitment to their children. The professionalism and confidence you project at Back-to-School Night can be instrumental toward getting parents on your side. Back-to-School Night can be a solitary event, unrelated to the rest of the year, or it can be the beginning of a dynamic year in which you and parents team up to become partners in their children's education. It all depends upon how you plan and deliver.

Unfortunately, we know that more than half of all parents don't attend Back-to-School Night. You may find that the very parents you want and need most to attend are the ones who don't show up. Don't just accept this; take action. Make a commitment to do all you can to encourage full parent participation. Use a variety of techniques to motivate parents to attend.

This chapter will outline the following ideas to help you plan and implement a great event:

- Remove logistical problems that may keep parents from attending.

- Send Back-to-School Night invitations.

- Involve students in planning.

- Use parent motivators to boost attendance.

- Reach out to parents who cannot come.

- Plan the classroom environment.

- Know exactly what you will say to parents.

- Present special Back-to-School Night activities.

- Keep the spirit alive.

Remove logistical problems that may keep parents from attending.

Some parents may not attend Back-to-School Night because they have other commitments. Try to accommodate parents' work schedules (if you are aware of them) and make sure that Back-to-School Night is set for a day and time that most parents are likely to be available.

Many parents cannot get away at night because they do not have a baby-sitter. Work with your administrators to set up a school-wide baby-sitting service for Back-to-School Night and you will see better attendance. Make sure that all parents are informed of the service.

If transportation to and from school has been a problem that kept parents from attending Back-to-School Night, set up a school-wide carpool service. Make sure all parents are aware of this service.

Send Back-to-School Night invitations.

Make sure parents receive personalized invitations from you. Let them know that you are really counting on their attendance and that Back-to-School Night is an important responsibility for both of you. Use the invitation to publicize some of the events planned and, most important, list compelling reasons why parents should attend. Include a tear-off RSVP portion that will encourage parents to commit to attending. Be sure to send this invitation well in advance, so that parents can make plans. Send a follow-up reminder a few days before. Invitations can be sent via email as well.

Involve students in planning.

Students at any grade level can help you create an inviting classroom atmosphere by designing "Welcome Parents" signs and other classroom posters or displays for Back-to-School Night. In addition, try to involve students in

Sample Back-to-School Night Invitation

To: _____

You're invited to **Back-to-School Night!**

Place _____

Date _____

Time _____

➤ See what we're doing in class.
➤ Learn what you can do at home to help your child be successful in school!
➤ Participate in the Back-to-School Night raffle! Prizes!
➤ Enjoy a video/slide presentation starring your child!
➤ Take home a **FREE** Parent Handbook filled with great ideas for you and your child.

Please join us.

Working Together We Can Make a Difference!

Baby-sitting will be available in Room 10.

- -

For carpool information, please call 555-5555.

❑ I will be attending Back-to-School Night.

❑ I won't be able to attend Back-to-School Night.

Name _____

Parent of _____

preparing some of your Back-to-School Night activities or presentations. (See pages 68 to 70 for suggestions.) By doing so, you will generate enthusiasm they will pass on to parents.

Use parent motivators to boost attendance.

Your first Back-to-School Night objective is to get parents there. To boost parent attendance, you may have to offer a few incentives. Try some of these ideas.

Hold a Back-to-School Night raffle.

Attending parents get to place signed raffle tickets in a jar. During a subsequent school day, the teacher pulls out several raffle tickets and gives prizes to the winning students. School supplies (markers, pocket dictionary, compass) make excellent prizes. Inform parents of the raffle ahead of time. And be sure to tell students, too, so they can help motivate their parents to participate.

Play Back-to-School Night lotto.

Each parent who attends Back-to-School Night writes his name in a space on a special Back-to-School Night lotto board. Later, in school, the teacher pulls the winning numbers and awards prizes to students whose parents' names were drawn.

Give Back-to-School Night bonus tickets.

Any student whose parent(s) attends Back-to-School Night receives a ticket entitling the student to a special privilege or award, such as free reading time, a pencil, or a notepad.

Reach out to parents who cannot come.

Some parents simply cannot come to Back-to-School Night. Others just choose not to come. Regardless of the reason, you owe it to yourself and your students to make another effort to contact them with your Back-to-School Night message.

The next day, send home any materials you distributed at Back-to-School Night. To avoid penalizing a student whose parents didn't attend, make sure you don't forget to give these parents a chance to participate in the raffle or lotto or any other incentive activity you used. Remember that you don't want to disenfranchise any parent. You want them all solidly behind you. Your willingness to go the extra mile will further demonstrate your commitment to all your students.

Sample Letter to Parents Who Did Not Attend

Dear Parent(s)

We missed you at Back-to-School Night.

I am sending you the Parent Handbook that I distributed at Back-to-School Night. It's filled with lots of information that will be useful as the year goes on. Please call me if you have any questions at all about anything in the handbook.

At Back-to-School Night, all the parents filled out raffle tickets for a classroom drawing. We will be having this drawing in a couple of days and students will win prizes such as pencils, rulers, and other school supplies. To make sure your child participates in the raffle, please fill out the coupon on the bottom of this letter and send it back to school as soon as possible.

- -

Back-to-School Night Raffle.

Working together we can make a difference!

Parent's name _____

Student's name _____

Plan the classroom environment.

First impressions really count at Back-to-School Night, so make a point of creating an environment that is inviting and friendly. You want parents to feel involved and welcomed. Let the room speak for you. Set the mood by hanging a bright "Welcome Parents" poster in the front of the room.

Here are other items that should be displayed:

- Class schedule (on board)

- Displays of students' work completed and curriculum in progress

- Centers or areas labeled clearly

Name tags help everybody get to know each other.

Introducing yourself to parents and parents to each other will be easier if everyone is wearing name tags. Put a supply of adhesive-backed tags near the classroom door and, as they enter, ask parents to write their names on the tags. You may wish to prepare name tags that leave a space for the student's name also. This will help you identify parents who may have a different last name than the student has. Name tags will help parents get acquainted with each other, too.

Know exactly what you will say to parents.

Be prepared. Know what you are going to say, when you are going to say it, and how you expect parents to participate. Back-to-School Night should be carefully orchestrated so that all your goals will be met. Make sure you prepare an outline of the topics you want to talk about with parents. This is no time to get nervous and leave out important information. It's perfectly okay (and a smart idea) to refer to note cards as you speak.

Your Back-to-School Night goal should be to convince parents of two things:

- Parents are the most important people in a child's life and, as such, are in a unique position to help children achieve their highest potential.

- You as their teacher sincerely care about the children and are committed to seeing them succeed.

Everything you say or do should be geared to achieving these goals. Always remember that communication is more than words. Make sure that your body language conveys your love for teaching, your interest in your students, and your confidence in your ability to make the upcoming year a success for everyone, academically and personally. (See Chapter 9 for more information on using body language in your communication with parents.) Smile, share stories about your students, create a good laugh, and show your enthusiasm.

Following are the major points that should be included in your Back-to-School Night presentation. If any of your student's parents are non-English speaking, make sure you have a translator available. Remember to look directly at parents as you speak, even when using a translator. Smile, make eye contact, and project the confidence you want the parents to feel.

Emphasize to parents that they are the most important people in their child's life.

Make sure you emphasize that research has proved over and over again that the best schools, the best teachers, and the best principals are not as important to a child's achievement in school as a parent is. Let them know that it is for this very reason that you want to work with them to educate their children. Make sure they know that you find their input, support, and backing extremely important and valuable.

Explain when and how you will communicate with parents.

Tell parents that you intend to communicate with them regularly. Explain that you will let them know when their children are successful. Say that you will also contact them if their children are not doing as well as they could. Explain that regular parent contact is central to your teaching plan because you firmly believe that when parent and teacher and student are working together, every student can be successful.

Invite parents to contact you.

Show parents that you are accessible. Emphasize that for you communication is a two-way street. Communication is cooperation. Invite parents to contact you with concerns, problems, and suggestions. Mention your office hours, but emphasize that parents should feel free to contact you at any time. Give out your email address, unless you are uncomfortable doing so.

Describe your classroom discipline plan.

Discuss your discipline plan to ensure parents that you will deal with student misbehavior fairly and consistently. Make sure parents know that supportive feedback is as central to your discipline plan as are corrective actions. Refer to the copy of the plan you already sent home. Allow parents to ask questions regarding your plan and, if necessary, explain your rationale. Make sure they know that the behavior management techniques you use are meant to keep your classroom safe and conducive to learning. Emphasize that the goal of your discipline plan is to help your students self-monitor their behavior in order to be more successful.

Describe your homework policy.

Refer to the copy of your homework policy you sent home for parents to read. Emphasize that homework is a meaningful way to increase the learning effect of any curriculum. Make sure parents know that you will enlist their help if problems arise. Show your confidence that homework can and will be a positive experience for students and parents.

Tell parents what you need from them.

Make sure parents know that you need and expect the following from them.

- Support for your academic efforts: Ask parents to let their children know that education is important to them.

- Support for your disciplinary efforts: Ask parents to communicate to their children that they expect them to follow the established classroom rules. Ask parents to follow up with appropriate disciplinary measures at home.

- Support for your homework policy: Ask parents to make sure that their children take homework seriously. Parents should see that their children have a quiet place to do homework, set a time when homework has to be done every day, and enforce and encourage doing homework with disciplinary techniques such as providing support and rewards and corrective actions.

Make sure parents understand that their support is in their children's best interest. Emphasize that they are the most important people in their children's lives.

Convey your confidence.

Express your firm belief that the cooperation between parents and teacher will make the coming year positive for students, parents, and teachers. If everyone does his share, the students will succeed.

Listen, take notes, and be ready with further suggestions.

As you speak, be sure to pause occasionally and ask parents if they have any questions or suggestions. Take notes on what is asked, on what parents suggest, or on any other issues that may arise. You should respond to all these concerns in a Back-to-School Night follow-up letter (see page 71). It's important to let parents know you are listening to them and that you take their concerns and suggestions seriously.

Here are some other points you may want to include in your presentation.

Give parents suggestions for how they can help at home.

Remember that parents often don't help their children with schoolwork because they just don't know what to do. Be prepared to give parents some specific ideas for helping their children at home. If, for example, students are beginning to print, send home a manuscript letter practice sheet. If students are learning multiplication facts, send home copies of flash cards that can be cut out. If students will soon be tackling a term paper, give the parents guidelines for helping with that project. Be sure to explain to parents how these materials are to be used. Follow up throughout the year with "helping at home" updates as the curriculum changes.

Introduce parents to power reading.

Reading comprehension skills are the basis for success in all subject areas. Parents can help their children develop these skills at home with the power reading technique. Here's how to introduce it.

> First, read aloud to your child for five minutes. Be sure that the book from which you are reading is at your child's reading level. Model good reading for them by

pronouncing words carefully and clearly, and by making appropriate pauses for periods and commas.

Next, listen to your child read aloud from the same book for another five minutes. Your child should begin at the point where you stopped reading. Remind your child to take it slowly and read so that the words make sense. This is why your oral reading is so important. It's setting an example for your child. Don't stop and correct your child while he is reading.

Finally, ask questions about what was read. Check how well your child was listening and reading by asking general questions about the material you read aloud and the material your child read aloud. Talk about the story together.

Power reading is an excellent way to improve reading skills and demonstrate the importance you place on reading. Start a book that is of particular interest to your child and continue using the same book for Power Reading sessions until it is completed.

Send parents home with a power reading tip sheet in which you outline the guidelines.

Invite parents to help at school.

Volunteers can be a great help to you in your classroom. Do some recruiting at Back-to-School Night. Think about the kind of help you would like to receive from parents, then put together a volunteer request letter. Make sure you offer some creative alternatives for working parents who can't be in the classroom during the school day (they like to help, too). Ideas might include creating posters for the classroom or helping out on a Saturday classroom improvement project. Don't hesitate to ask parents what they'd like to do; you just might have a talented storyteller, musician, puppeteer, scientist, or chef among them.

Present special Back-to-School Night activities.

You've encouraged parents to attend, created an inviting atmosphere, and spoken to them with assurance and clarity. Don't let it end there. There are other activities that you can incorporate into Back-to-School Night that will round out the evening and help make a lasting impression. Below are some effective suggestions that can make the event an even greater success.

Take parents on a tour of the classroom.

Parents are interested in what their children are learning at school, so take this opportunity to show off your classroom. Don't assume that parents understand the reasons behind your classroom organization and materials. Explain everything. Let them know why you have a listening center filled with a jumble of headsets (for individualized instruction). Explain the reason for the hamster cage (to teach responsibility). Point out your classroom library with pride and tell the parents how it will be used. Explain to parents that the classroom and its contents will be the students' learning laboratory for a year. Get the parents excited about it. Your educational plans will come alive for parents if they are given the opportunity to feel a part of them. Encourage parents to ask questions about anything they see.

Give parents a "private screening."

All parents love to see their children (whatever their age) in a starring role. Present a slide or video presentation showing students in their daily classroom routines—entering the classroom, working in small groups, doing independent seat work, moving to centers, etc. Don't forget a group shot of the entire class. Make sure every student appears in the slide show. This will communicate to parents that you really do care about all your students.

Make tape recordings.

Play a tape recording of students discussing classroom activities. Have elementary students tape record a song to be played for parents.

Have students write notes to parents.

Have each student write a note to the parents to be left in the student's desk. (In upper grades, the notes could be kept in a class folder and distributed to parents.) At Back-to-School Night, the parents read the notes and write a return message to their child. In elementary grades, the parents' notes can be left for students on their own desks.

Create and distribute a Parent Handbook.

Hand out a packet of information that parents can take home with them. This Parent Handbook is a convenient way to give parents a lot of information in one package. Here is a list of items you might want to include:

- Class roster (It's especially helpful for parents of primary children to know the names of their child's classmates.)

- School staff list, address, phone number, hours, email address(es), website address

- Map of the school

- School-wide rules

- Discipline plan (if not sent in a separate letter)

- Daily classroom schedule

- Grade level curriculum

- Manuscript or cursive writing guide

- School/calendar year showing all school holidays and other school closures

- Blank teacher/parent communication forms

- Policies about absences, medical appointments, making up class work

- Tips on how to help a child study at home

- Suggested reading lists

- Power reading tip sheet

- Health concerns (nutrition, exercise, or sleep)

Write the name of each student on a Parent Handbook. After Back-to-School Night, send home to parents the handbooks that were not picked up at school.

Keep the spirit alive.

Don't let the enthusiasm generated by Back-to-School Night just fade away. Use it to your advantage. Let parents know how much you appreciated their participation. A few days afterward, send a brief note home thanking parents for attending. Update them on any items that might have come under discussion at Back-to-School Night. And, because it's sometimes difficult for parents to speak up and air their concerns in front of a whole group, you might also include a "return message" section where parents can write back to you with any questions they may have. This follow-up note is also an excellent way to make contact with parents who did not attend Back-to-School Night.

The sense of teamwork, camaraderie, and excitement you cultivate at Back-to-School Night is a great way to help parents overcome the roadblocks that keep them from giving you support. By doing so, you will also increase your own confidence in just how successful you can be in getting parents on your side.

Making the Most of Back-to-School Night
REMINDERS

DO

➤ Plan your Back-to-School Night schedule as thoroughly as you would a day in class.

➤ Have translators available if necessary.

➤ Speak to every parent. Call them by name and refer to their child by name (name tags can help make this easier).

➤ Plan what you will say. Keep your notes with you as you speak.

➤ Provide a program that allows each student to be highlighted in some way (show photographs, tape recordings, a video, class work, artwork).

➤ Focus on the responsibility of parent and teacher to work as partners in children's education.

➤ Encourage parents to offer their special talents and interests to the classroom as the year goes on.

➤ Listen to parents. Take notes about any questions or concerns that are brought up. Follow up on these concerns.

➤ Provide relevant, informative material for parents to take home.

➤ Reach out to parents who didn't attend. Send all Back-to-School Night materials home the next day.

➤ Send out a Back-to-School Night follow-up letter.

(continued)

Making the Most of Back-to-School Night
REMINDERS *(continued)*

DON'T

➤ Don't expect parents to come just because the school sent home a notice. Reach out to them. It's up to you to get the parents of your students there.

➤ Don't talk only about curriculum. Remember that your first goal should be to convince parents of the important role they play in their children's education.

➤ Don't talk down to parents or be intimidated by them. Approach them as equals, but keep in mind that you are the professional educator.

➤ Don't make the mistake of thinking that exciting Back-to-School Nights are for elementary classes only. Parents of older students also appreciate a motivating presentation.

Making the Most of Back-to-School Night
CHECKLIST

Refer to this checklist as you plan your Back-to-School Night.

Have you:

____ sent home invitations to parents that explain why Back-to-School Night is so important?

____ planned to use a "parent motivator" to help get parents to attend?

____ written down what you want to say to parents?

____ created a welcoming environment in your classroom?

____ created a Parent Handbook to give to parents at Back-to-School Night?

____ decided on the activities you will present?

____ arranged for a translator if necessary?

____ decided to send a Back-to-School Night follow-up letter to parents?

Establishing Positive Communication With Parents

Show you care. For effective teachers, these are really words to live by. Every day, all year long, positive communication is imperative to show that you care and to get past the roadblocks that keep parents from supporting their children at school. Parents see educators who consistently communicate positive news to them as educators who truly care about their children. And the more parents feel you care, the more they will listen and support you. Unless you are prepared to pursue consistent positive communication with parents, you will have a difficult time getting all the parents on your side.

In this chapter, you will learn some proven techniques teachers use for positive communication with parents. You will learn how to do the following:

- Place positive phone calls.

- Send notes, cards, and letters.

- Make home visits.

- Plan parent communication activities.

- Keep a record of positive contacts.

If you are a middle school or secondary school teacher, don't let the large number of students you teach deter you from making positive contact with parents. In upper grades, the best way to reach every parent is through a school-wide plan in which all teachers work together so that all parents receive regular, planned positive contact. Design a simple schedule according to which every teacher is assigned a group of students whose parents should be contacted as soon as there is something positive to report. Such a schedule should rotate students among teachers at least twice a year.

Of course, establishing such a schedule may prove too cumbersome at your school. Even if you're on your own, you can still reach out to parents regularly.

Careful planning is the answer. You'd be surprised at the number of students you can reach if you just schedule time for positives. A quick positive phone call, for example, is easy to make and takes only a couple of minutes. Make two brief calls each afternoon and you've reached 10 parents a week. Multiply that by 36 weeks and you've reached 360 parents. As you read about the positive communication techniques in this chapter, give thought to how you could schedule them into your week. Then set a goal of reaching a specific number of parents each week.

Above all, keep this in mind: It won't happen if you don't schedule it.

Place positive phone calls.

One of the most effective parent communication techniques at your disposal is a quick phone call home to let parents know how well their child is doing. It doesn't have to be a long conversation—just a brief update and a few friendly words. Get into the habit of phoning parents with good news and it won't be so difficult to call them when there is a problem to be solved. You will have already established a comfortable relationship, and parents will be much more likely to listen to what you have to say.

Try to make these calls at a time when you are most likely to reach the parents. For example, call working parents in the evenings or on Saturday mornings. If you only reach voice mail, don't just hang up—leave a message. Parents will be delighted to come home to a positive message.

Plan exactly what you will say.

Here are the points you'll want to cover in a positive phone call.

1. **Describe the student's positive behavior.**
   Begin the call by telling the parent the specific behavior the student exhibited in your classroom.

   "Brandon is off to a great start this semester. He's completed all his class assignments and homework this week."

2. **Describe how you feel about the student's positive behavior.**
   Let the parent know how pleased you are with the student's good behavior or academic performance. Remember that this may be the first time the parent has heard anything positive about her child in a long time.

"I'm very pleased that Doug is showing such improvement in math this year. His hard work is getting results."

3. **Ask the parent to share the content of the conversation with the student.** Your conversation with the parent will have an even greater impact if the parent tells the child about the call. It is important for the student to know that both you and the parent are proud of her accomplishments.

    "When Tonya gets home, please share our conversation with her. I think it will be great for her to know that I called and how pleased we both are with her performance in school."

Sample Phone Conversation

Here's a sample positive phone conversation.

Teacher:	Mrs. Suarez, this is Mrs. Endicott, José's math teacher. I just wanted to let you know how well José is doing in school. He is a really hard worker. He gets right to work on all of his assignments, follows directions beautifully, and always seems to do the best job he can.
Parent:	Well, he does seem to be enjoying school more this year.
Teacher:	I'm glad to hear that. I really enjoy having him in my classroom.
Parent:	I appreciate your telling me this. It's really made my day!
Teacher:	Well, I believe it's just as important to tell parents when their child is doing well in school as it is when the child is having problems.
Parent:	That makes sense to me.
Teacher:	It makes sense to me, too. There's one last thing. Please let José know that I called and how happy I am about how well he's doing in class. I want to be sure he knows that his good work is noticed by all of us.
Parent:	I sure will! Thank you!

Send notes, cards, and letters.

The school year will be filled with occasions that call for positive parent communication. Take advantage of as many of these "good news" opportunities as possible.

In many cases, you may want to use email to send a quick note or a birthday or get-well greeting.

Write positive notes to parents.

An effective way to give parents supportive feedback on their child's performance in school is to send home positive notes. A positive note consists of a few lines mentioning some good news about their child. Once you get into the habit of sending home a predetermined number of notes each week, it will become a natural part of your routine. And this habit will pay dividends: It will be much easier to contact parents about a problem if they've already heard from you in a positive context.

- Keep a file of ready-to-use positive notes and preaddressed envelopes in your desk. Save ready-to-use notes in your computer, too.

- Plan to send home a specific number of notes each week.

- When writing notes, address the parents by name and mention the student's name, too. Keep the notes brief and to the point.

Sample Positive Note

October 14

Dear Mr. and Mrs. Brown,

Just wanted to let you know what a terrific job Kiana did today in giving her oral report to the class. Her presentation was both informative and entertaining. You should be proud of the good work she is doing!

Sincerely,

Mr. Smith

Send home good behavior messages and academic awards.

In addition to personalized notes, send home behavior messages or academic awards to parents. Many of these awards are commercially available with a preprinted message ("Thought you'd like to know that _____'s behavior in class today was terrific!"). All you have to do is add the child's name and send the award home with the student.

The spotlight is on YOU for good behavior!

Send birthday greetings.

Add your good wishes to birthday celebrations by sending home greetings to students on their special day.

For students: What better way to let parents know that you care about their child than by sending home a birthday card. When it arrives in the mail, everyone in the family sees that you do care. If you have access to a computer and printer, you can easily run off cards that are personalized both with words and graphics. Keep a class birthday list in your plan book so that you can be prepared.

For parents: Have students create a birthday card for each parent as an art project at the beginning of the year. File them away by date and send home when appropriate.

Send get-well cards and make phone calls.

When students are sick, parents are worried, work schedules are upset, and life becomes more complicated for families. This is a good opportunity to show your concern for your student and his parents. When a student is sick for more than a few days, send home a get-well card. Pick up the phone or send a quick email to see how the child is doing. You can also use this opportunity to update the parent on the child's class work.

Here's an example of a get-well phone call.

"Mrs. Lee? Hi. This is Sandra Hyatt, David's teacher. We've missed David this week and I just wanted to give you a call and see how he's doing. The whole class sends their best wishes. We're looking forward to having him back.

"I know he may be concerned about the work he's missing, but tell him to concentrate on getting well! I'll work with him on catching up when he's feeling better."

Write thank-you notes.

Throughout the year, parents will help you in many ways: donating supplies to the classroom, volunteering time, chaperoning field trips or dances, or helping their child with a project. Don't let these good deeds go unrecognized. Parents will be more motivated to help out again if they feel that their contribution was appreciated. Keep a supply of thank-you notes on hand and use them often. Students too will notice and feel proud when these acknowledgments go home.

Each Friday spend a few minutes reviewing the week. Jot down the names of parents who made that special effort you appreciate and send home a note to each.

Make home visits.

Nothing is quite as personal, or demonstrates your concern and caring, as a visit to a student's home. This is especially true when the purpose of a home visit is simply to say hello, meet the family, and talk to the parent about the positive things the student is doing in school. A home visit can be a wonderful experience for student, parent, and teacher. For the parent, it's an opportunity to meet the teacher in comfortable, familiar, and relaxed surroundings. For the student, it's a chance to clearly see that home and school are a team that's working together. For you, a home visit can give you a better perspective on a student's life away from school.

You will find that once you have met personally with parents under such positive circumstances, it will be all the easier to contact them about any problems that arise as the year proceeds.

- Try to make as many home visits as you can at the start of the year.

- Be sure to call the parent ahead of time to schedule a date and time for the visit. Don't just drop in!

Plan parent communication activities.

When parents are connected with what's going on in your classroom, it will be easier for you to stay connected with them. Keep parents informed about school-work and other classroom activities.

Create a daily "school-to-home" journal.

When parents ask their child, "What happened in school today?" the answer is often, "Nothing." You can encourage better public relations than this. A daily journal that goes back and forth between home and school can keep parents and students communicating. At the end of each day, have students write a few sentences telling what went on in school that day. Each night, have students take the journals home to be read by their parents. Have parents sign the day's entry, and have the student return the journal to school.

Send home a weekly envelope containing student work.

The more a parent knows about a child's work at school, the higher the probability you will get the support you need. Plan to send home a folder or large envelope each Friday containing student work from the previous week. Label the folder "Special Delivery to Parents." The folder should include space for the parents to sign, indicating that they looked at the child's work. You may also wish to include space for parents to make comments. Students should be instructed to return the folder to school on Monday. (Positive notes and awards can be sent home in the folders, too.)

Compose a weekly classroom newsletter.

Send home a newsletter each week informing parents about classroom activities and upcoming events. Newsletters can also be posted on the school's website. Make sure that your students do some, if not most, of the work on the newsletter. This method of communication will be most effective if students help create it.

Here are two newsletter ideas.

Weekly Family Letter (for primary grades)
Every Friday, each student writes three or more sentences telling what he did during that week. The sentences are turned in, and the teacher compiles them

into one big letter (typed), making sure that at least one sentence from each child is included. The letter is addressed to "Dear Family." On Monday, the teacher gives each student a copy of the letter. Students mark what they wrote on their copy and take it home to show to proud parents.

Suggestions for use: Send home a note to parents with the first Weekly Family Letter. Make sure they understand that this letter will be a weekly group effort and that their child's writing will be included each week. Suggest that they ask their child to read the whole letter to them each week and to spend some time talking about the events recorded in the letter.

Keep all the weekly letters in a three-ring binder. As the weeks go by, students will enjoy looking back at their classroom experiences. You may wish to occasionally include photographs to add further interest to this very lively history.

Family Newsletter (for upper grades)

Older students will enjoy having a hand in planning and producing a weekly (or biweekly) newsletter. As a class project, decide on regular columns that will be included in the newsletter. Assign committees to be responsible for gathering the information for and writing each column. Rotate assignments throughout the year.

Suggestions for columns:

A Message from the Teacher
We're Proud of These Students!
Upcoming Projects and Assignments
Special Events
Opinion Poll
What We Need (what parents can do specifically to help the class or school)

Keep a record of positive contacts.

Because you want to be sure that all students and parents are receiving equal, positive attention, it's important to keep track of the calls you make and the notes and awards you send home. Set up a column in your roll book or plan book to record this information. List each student's name. When a note or award goes home, or a phone call is made, jot down the date on the line next to the name. Get into the habit of reviewing this list regularly.

While you should not ignore the achievements of high-performing students, bear in mind that it is extremely important to send home positive notes to parents of students with potential academic or behavior problems, or to parents of students who have had problems in the past. The more the parents of these children hear good news, the greater the probability of getting their support when you need it. Also, recognizing a difficult student for a positive achievement may even help this student to stay on track and keep up the good work.

Establishing Positive Communication with Parents
REMINDERS

DO

➤ Make special effort to communicate positively with parents of students who have had problems in the past.

➤ Set goals for sending home a specific number of positive notes each week.

➤ Make positive home visits at the start of the year, and all year long.

➤ Keep track of all parent communications.

➤ Phone parents with positive updates on academic and behavior successes.

➤ Keep the positive momentum going all year long.

DON'T

➤ Don't underestimate how important positive notes and phone calls to parents are. They really do want to hear good news from you.

➤ Don't forget to give positive reinforcement to the students who always behave and do their work. They shouldn't be ignored.

➤ Don't forget to say thank-you to parents any time they help you out.

➤ Don't make negative communication the first contact you have with parents.

Establishing Positive Communication with Parents
CHECKLIST

Refer to this checklist as you plan positive communication with parents.

Have you:

___ set goals for sending home positive notes to parents? How many notes will you plan to send home each week?

___ started making positive phone calls to parents? Once you try it, you'll like it. It's easy, effective, and always welcomed.

___ made a birthday list of students and set aside birthday cards so you'll always be prepared?

___ put together a collection of get-well cards and thank-you notes for use throughout the year?

___ set up a record-keeping system to keep track of your positive communications?

___ planned to send home a classroom newsletter to keep parents informed about what's going on in your classroom?

Involving Parents in the Homework Process

Homework has the potential to be the most consistent day-to-day contact you can have with parents, particularly in the upper elementary grades and in secondary school. Yet parents complain that homework is often the greatest cause of conflict between them and their children. Likewise, teachers complain that students don't complete assignments and parents won't follow up to see that they do. The result is that in most classrooms an important parent involvement resource goes to waste. Changing homework from an irritant into a positive is what you will find in this chapter.

Too often, homework remains a mystery to parents. They don't understand why homework is given, when it will be given, how it is expected to be done, or what they can do to help. In short, parents' responsibilities in the homework process are usually never really addressed. All they know for sure about homework is that it's often a problem. This is unfortunate for both parent and student because the homework process also has the potential to increase a student's self-esteem. When parent and child work together, the child knows that he is important enough for the parent to stop what she's doing, pay attention, and get involved. And that's a good feeling for a child to have.

Teachers who are committed to involving parents in the homework process start by developing a homework policy. The policy establishes a firm foundation for homework by stating the expectations of everyone involved—students, parents, and teacher. Your homework policy is just the beginning, though. You need to follow through all year long by keeping parents well informed about class work, upcoming tests and projects, and ways in which they can help their children study more successfully.

This chapter covers four ways you can turn homework into an asset of your parent involvement plan:

- Help parents help their children do a better job on homework.

- Keep the lines of communication open.

- Assign family learning activities on weekends.

- Help parents solve their children's most common homework problems.

Help parents help their children do a better job on homework.

Most parents want to help their children do well with homework, but they don't know how or where to begin. Start off the year by providing parents with useful homework and study skills tips so they can begin immediately to improve their child's homework performance.

Plan to send homework and study skills tip sheets home at the beginning of the school year. (Guidelines for creating the tip sheets follow. Some sample sheets are also included.) When preparing the tip sheets and distributing them to your students' parents, use these guidelines:

- Each study skills and homework tip should be self-contained on its own page. Include as much specific information as possible.

- Rather than send all study skills and homework tips home at once, you may choose instead to send specific tips home in correlation with assigned work.

Homework and study skills tips should also accommodate a particular child's personal learning style. Often a child exhibits a learning style different from that of his parents. This may cause problems between parents and students that significantly hamper the success of your homework policy. If this is the case, make sure you assist the parents in understanding and accommodating their child's personal needs. Help the parents understand that not everybody learns best in the same way: Some children may study better lying on the floor rather than sitting at a desk; some may concentrate best while listening to soft music.

Accepting and supporting a child's own learning style may help the child to learn about his strengths and weaknesses, which help or hinder his achievements in class. Accepting and supporting a child's own learning style may help the child accept his own personality as unique, which in turn may increase his self-esteem.

Accommodating a child's learning style should not be taken as an excuse for accepting distractions. Phone calls, television, and noisy interruptions by siblings or friends are not part of a calming work environment.

Give parents homework tips.

Good homework habits must be developed if a student is to do homework successfully. These five homework tips will guide parents in helping their children organize and complete homework each night.

Homework Tip #1:
Set up a study area.
To do homework successfully, a student must have a place at home in which to work. The study area must be well lit, quiet, and have all necessary supplies close at hand. The study area should accommodate the student's particular learning style. For example, if the student needs absolute quiet to concentrate, nobody else should be allowed in the area while the student is doing his homework.

Homework Tip #2:
Create a homework survival kit.
Students can waste a lot of time in last-minute frenzied searches for homework supplies. Parents can put together a homework survival kit for their children that contains all the usual materials the children might need to complete their homework assignments. These materials can include pens, pencils, pencil sharpener, paper, ruler, scissors, and glue.

Homework Tip #3:
Schedule daily homework time.
Probably the touchiest homework issue students deal with is finding the time to do homework. Every parent knows that kids will find time for sports, TV, and talking on the telephone, but somehow time runs out when homework needs to be done. Parents can help their children schedule daily homework time and get them to stick to it. It is best if the student is encouraged to do her homework as soon as possible after school and at a time when parents are available to help if necessary.

Homework Tip #4:
Encourage children to work independently.

Homework teaches students responsibility. Through homework, students learn skills they must develop if they are to grow to be independent, successful adults. Parents should encourage their children to work on their own. In other words, parents should only offer help once all resources for independent work have been used. Parents should encourage their children to use reference books and dictionaries to collect information. Parents should encourage their children to call a friend with questions before they ask parents for help. Attempting to use resources other than a parent to complete homework will help the student to develop creative problem-solving skills.

Homework Tip #5:
Motivate children with praise.

Because children need encouragement and support from the people whose opinions they value the most, praise is the best motivational tool parents can use. Consistent praise can increase a child's self-confidence, develop a sense of pride in personal achievements, and motivate him to do the best work possible.

Give parents study skills tips.

Knowing how to study is an important part of successful learning. But good study habits don't just happen. They must be taught in school and reinforced at home.

Give parents guidelines for helping their child in three key study areas: long-range planning, writing reports, and studying for tests. Send these study skills tips home only if appropriate to the ages and needs of your students. (Samples of tip sheets you might prepare for parents are provided.)

Study Skills Tip #1:
Provide help with long-range planning.

Assignments such as book reports, written reports, and science projects are often overwhelming for students (and parents) because they require advance planning and time management. Because students usually don't know how to structure their time, the bulk of the work is often left until the last minute. Give parents a long-range planner, and guidelines for helping their child use it.

A long-range planner can help students break down a big assignment into smaller tasks. Ask parents to take time to help their children determine the steps

Sample Study Skills Tip: Long-Range Planner

Long-Range Planner

Directions:

1. Break down your big assignments into smaller steps.

2. Write down your due dates for each step.

3. Fill in the final due date for the project on your last step.

Assignment _____   **Due Date** _____

_____

1. _____   Due Date _____

_____

2. _____   Due Date _____

_____

3. _____   Due Date _____

_____

4. _____   Due Date _____

_____

5. _____   Due Date _____

_____

6. _____   Due Date _____

_____

7. _____   Due Date _____

_____

that have to be followed to complete the project, then to establish the date each step will be completed. If each goal is met, there will be no last-minute panic before the report is due.

Study Skills Tip #2:
Provide help with written reports.
Written reports are often difficult for students to handle in an organized manner. Here are three suggestions for parents that can make the job easier:

1. Use a long-range planner (instructions provided in Study Skills Tip #1).

2. Use a written report checklist. A written report checklist should address the length of the report, the format and style you expect the report to follow, as well as whether you expect illustrations or other additional materials.

3. Use a proofreading checklist (see page 94). Proofreading should be a part of every written assignment. The checklist should address such issues as grammar, spelling, organization of content, style, and effort.

Study Skills Tip #3:
Help your child study for a test.
Students can study more effectively if they learn how to manage their time and how to use study techniques specifically tailored for test taking. Provide parents with general tips on how to help their child prepare for studying, and specific tips for studying a textbook (see pages 95 and 96).

Keep the lines of communication open.

The guidelines in *Parents on Your Side* have emphasized the importance of consistent communication with parents. This is especially true with homework. Here are some ideas that can keep the home-school connection working effectively.

Institute a parent-teacher homework memo procedure.

When you need a reply to a homework question or problem, use a parent-teacher homework memo. Write your message on the top portion of the memo; ask parents to respond on the lower part and return the memo to you. You may wish to send parents a supply of memos at the beginning of the school year,

Sample Study Skills Tip: Written Report Checklist

Written Report Checklist

Directions:

When a report is assigned, write or check off the requirements below.

Subject of Report: _____

Date Report Is Due: _____

1. How long should the report be? How many paragraphs ____ or pages ____ do I need to write?

2. Should the report be typewritten or handwritten?
    Typewritten ❑   Pen ❑   Pencil ❑

3. Should I write on every line or every other line?
    Every line ❑   Every other line ❑

4. Should I write on one side of the page or both?
    One side ❑   Both sides ❑

5. Where should I put the page numbers?
    Top ❑   Bottom ❑

6. Should I put the report in a folder?
    Yes ❑   No ❑

7. Should I add photos or illustrations?
    Photos ❑   Illustrations ❑

Other: _____

_____

_____

Additional Notes: _____

_____

_____

_____

_____

Sample Study Skills Tip: Proofreading Checklist

Proofreading Checklist

Directions:

Use this checklist each time you complete a draft of your report.

Subject of Report: _____

Date Report Is Due: _____

____ The title of the paper is suited to the subject.

____ The paper is well organized and the introduction is clear.

____ I have put in all capital letters, commas, periods, and apostrophes.

____ Every sentence is a complete sentence.

____ Each paragraph has a topic sentence that tells what the paragraph will be about.

____ I have used descriptive words to make my paper more interesting.

____ The paper contains specific information about the subject.

____ I have read my paper aloud and it says what I want it to say.

____ The last sentence lets the reader know the paper is finished.

____ I have completed at least one rough draft of the paper.

____ I have checked the paper for spelling errors.

____ This is my best work.

Sample Study Skills Tip: How to Help Your Child Study for a Test

How to Help Your Child Study for a Test

Whenever an upcoming test is announced, follow these steps to help get your child off to a good start.

1. **Determine what the test will cover and organize all study materials.**

   Help your child find out exactly what material a test will cover: chapters in a textbook, class notes, homework assignments, etc. Make sure they are available for study.

2. **Schedule time for studying ahead of time.**

   Don't allow your child to wait until the last minute to study. Break down study tasks throughout the week. It is better to study a little bit each day than to cram the night before a test.

3. **Use effective study techniques.**

   ➤ As your child studies, he should write important information on index cards. Later, these cards can be used to review for the test.

   ➤ Review homework and class notes. It is helpful to underline or highlight important points.

   ➤ Review study questions and past quizzes and tests. Also, make sure your child reviews study questions in the textbook, which provide an excellent review of material covered.

along with a letter encouraging them to write whenever they have a homework-related question they would like to discuss with you.

Send home positive homework notes to parents.

Just as you send positive notes to parents about students' good behavior or academic success, you can also send home notes relating specifically to homework. These notes are especially effective if they relate to assignments parents

Sample Study Skills Tip: How to Help Your Child Study a Textbook

How to Help Your Child Study a Textbook

Often, the material covered on a test will be from assigned reading in the class textbook. Here is what you can do to help your child master the material in any textbook:

1. **Survey the chapter.**
   The first step in studying a textbook is to survey the chapter. Have your child follow these steps:

   ➤ Read all headings and subheadings.
   ➤ Look over all pictures, maps, charts, tables, and graphs.
   ➤ Read the summary at the end of the chapter.
   ➤ Read through the study questions listed at the end of the chapter.
   ➤ Finally, go back and make up a question from each main heading.

2. **Read the chapter and take notes.**
   After a survey of the chapter, your child should go back and read it all the way through. Notes should be taken on a separate sheet of paper. These notes should include answers to the questions made from the chapter headings, and a chronological listing of events that occur in the chapter.

   In addition, your child should take notes on index cards. Important facts (names of persons, terms to know, or significant concepts) are listed on the front of the card. The back should be used for listing important points that may be asked on the test.

3. **Review the chapter.**
   After reading the chapter, your child should look over the notes and make sure all the main points are understood. Then she should answer the study questions given at the end of the chapter, as well as the questions formulated from the main headings. Your child should review all the notes and all the key points of the chapter.

have been involved with, or if they address homework problems that have been solved.

For example:

"Just a note to let you know what a great job Austin did on his report on mammals. I know how much hard work he put into it. Thanks so much for helping him get the library books he needed!"

"Susan has turned in all of her math assignments during the past two weeks and she earned an A on her test today. Now she understands that doing homework makes a difference in how well she does on tests!"

As with other positive notes you send, follow these guidelines:

- Plan to send home a specific number of positive homework notes each week.

- Be specific. Tell the parent exactly what the student did to earn the note.

- Keep a record of notes sent home.

Give positive homework notes to students.

Students put lots of effort into homework. Let them know you both notice and appreciate the work they do. Pay particular attention to students who have improved their homework habits. Your praise will increase the likelihood that these new habits will continue.

"Terrific job on your outline. I can tell that you really used your resource materials."

"Thank you for writing so neatly. Now your stories are even more fun to read!"

Send home test update slips.

Students often forget to study for tests until the last minute, and parents sometimes hear about tests when it's too late to help their children study. Test update slips can help both student and parent to prepare for tests. Send home these notices well in advance of important tests. Have both the student and parent sign the slips and return them to class. This form of home-school communication can be a very positive force in promoting good study habits.

Encourage the use of homework assignment books.

Assignment books ensure that students write down all homework and that parents have an opportunity to see what those assignments are. Students keep the assignment book in their notebook, take it home each day, and bring it back the next day. If appropriate, you may ask parents to sign the assignment book each night, indicating that homework assignments have been completed.

Using an assignment book prevents students from saying that they don't know what their assignments are and ensures that the parents know exactly what is expected of their children each night.

For younger students, consider sending home a weekly homework calendar that lists all assignments for the week. It's easy for young children to forget their homework assignments. A homework calendar allows parents to check what's been assigned and what their child has completed.

Ask parents to sign completed homework.

Sometimes just asking a parent to sign completed homework assignments is enough to motivate students to finish them. Use this technique whenever you want to make sure a parent is checking a student's work.

Assign family learning activities on weekends.

Parent-child homework assignments can be worthwhile experiences for everyone. Yet few things are as frustrating to a parent as arriving home from work at night, exhausted, and finding out a child has an assignment that requires parental input and is due the next day. It's not fair to the parent, and it's not fair to the student. What should be a pleasant activity instead turns into a stressful duty.

Teachers often avoid assigning homework on the weekends, but maybe it's time to reassess. After all, many parents have more time to spend on a child's work during the weekend than they do during the week. Try this idea: Tell parents that students will be bringing home a weekend assignment once a month that will involve parents in some way. Explain your reasons for these assignments.

Sample Family Learning Activities Letter

Dear Parent(s):

Although it's important that students learn to do their homework on their own, I believe there are times when they can benefit from working with parents on a project. For this reason, I am planning to send home a variety of family learning activities throughout the year. These activities are designed to involve you and your child in a creative and interesting activity. I know you are busy, so I will let you know ahead of time when each assignment is coming. I will plan these assignments for weekends, when you and your child will have more time to do and enjoy them. It is my hope that these activities will be fun for everyone.

Sincerely,

Mrs. Wilkinson

Try these ideas for family learning activities.

Smart Shopper
Go to the grocery store together. Pretend you have $25.00 to spend. Your job is to plan a lunch and dinner for four people. Make sure each meal is well balanced. Write down the menu and the cost of each item you will have to buy.

Walk 'n' Talk
Go on a walk in your neighborhood with a parent. Together, write down 10 things you see, 10 things you smell, 10 things you hear, and 10 things you touch.

Finders Keepers
Using items found at home, work with your parent to create

- something funny to look at;

- something that can move forward;

- the tallest structure you can make that still balances;

- a structure that is 4 inches high and 3 inches wide.

Speak Out!
Interview your parent to find out about _____.
  For example:

- Your family tree

- Her opinion of the United Nations

- His favorite book

- What she would do in case of an emergency (such as an earthquake, tornado, or flood)

- His opinion about the best place in the world to live

Turn It On!
Watch a video or a TV show about Earth's environment on Saturday night.

  Parent: List 10 things you will do to help the environment.
  Student: List 10 things you will do to help the environment.

Read your lists to each other. Are any items the same? Decide on four things each of you will begin doing right away.
  NOTE: In consideration of different family situations, you may wish to offer a choice of three activities.

Help parents solve their children's most common homework problems.

When problems with homework persist and you can't solve them yourself, you need more involvement on the part of parents. Prepare parent resource sheets to use throughout the year to help parents deal with specific homework problems. The resource sheets offer a plan of action for parents to follow when

- children do not do their best work;

- children refuse to do their homework;

- children fail to bring home assignments;

- children take all night to finish homework;

- children will not do homework on their own;

- children wait until the last minute to finish assignments;

- children will not do homework if parents are not home.

Sample resource sheets are provided for all these topics. When you prepare your own, however, keep in mind that the sheets need to explain that parents should

- clearly and firmly state their homework expectations to the child;

- institute daily homework time (as explained on the resource sheets) and determine loss of privileges if the child still chooses not to do homework;

- give praise and supportive feedback for work well done;

- provide backup incentives for continued good work;

- back up their words with action;

- contact the teacher if all else fails.

How to use the parent resource sheets.

- When there is a homework-related problem you need help with, contact the parent by phone or make arrangements to get together in a face-to-face meeting.

- Together, determine the specific problem the child is having. For example: takes all night to get it done, forgets to bring assignments home. (Review the guidelines on pages 164 to 168 for conducting a problem-solving conference.)

- Select the appropriate resource sheet and together go over each of the steps to make sure the parent understands what is to be done. Give the parent a copy of the sheet to take home. Don't give the resource sheet to a parent if you feel that he will be intimidated by it. Instead, make sure the parent is given clear verbal guidelines to follow.

- Set a time (in a week or two) to follow up with the parent to determine whether the strategy has been effective or if further action is necessary.

Sample Parent Resource Sheet: What to Do When Your Child Does Not Do Her Best Work

Solving Homework Problems

What to Do When Your Child Does Not Do Her Best Work

If your child rushes through homework to talk on the phone, use the computer, watch TV, or get together with friends, state that it is not okay to do incomplete or sloppy work. Use these tips to help your child take responsibility for doing homework well.

1. **Schedule daily homework time.**
   Allot a time each day when all other activities stop and your child must go to her study area and do homework.

2. **Tell your child what you expect.**
   Say, "I know you can do a better job. I want you to take your time and do the best work you can. Sloppy work is not acceptable."

3. **Praise your child for work well done.**
   Say, "Great job getting your homework done," or "I like how neat your paper looks. Keep up the good work." Praise is the best way to encourage continued best efforts.

4. **Institute mandatory homework time.**
   This means that your child must use the entire scheduled daily homework time for homework or other academic activities whether or not homework is completed. For example, if two hours is allotted each night, the entire time must be spent on homework or, if homework is finished, on reading, reviewing textbooks, or practicing math. Your child will learn that nothing can be gained by rushing through homework and will be encouraged to slow down and do a better job.

5. **Provide additional incentives.**
   To encourage your child to continue good work, give a reward or a point toward a prize each time homework is completed. For example, when five points are earned, reward your child with an extra privilege.

6. **Contact the teacher.**
   If after trying these steps your child is still not doing her best work, you must work together with the teacher to improve your child's performance.

Sample Parent Resource Sheet: What to Do When Your Child Refuses to Do Homework

Solving Homework Problems

What to Do When Your Child Refuses to Do Homework

When your child would rather battle with you than do homework, it's time to set firm limits. Your child may openly refuse to do homework or lie to you or the teacher about why it hasn't been done. You must make it clear that choosing not to do homework is choosing not to enjoy certain privileges.

1. **State clearly how you expect homework to be completed.**
   Say, "I expect you to do all of your homework every night. Under no circumstances will I tolerate your refusing to do your assignments."

2. **Back up your words with action.**
   Say, "You can choose either to do your homework or to lose these privileges: You will not leave this house. You will not watch TV, listen to music, or use the telephone. You will sit here until all of your homework is done. The choice is yours." Stick to your demands. It may take your child several days to realize that you mean business.

3. **Praise your child when homework is completed.**
   Say, "You've been getting all of your homework done. You should feel proud of yourself."

4. **Use a homework contract.**
   This motivator is a written, signed agreement between you and your child that states a reward or a point toward a prize will be earned for each day that homework is brought home and completed. (The younger the child, the more quickly the prize is earned.)

5. **Contact the teacher.**
   If problems continue, request that additional discipline be provided at school for incomplete assignments. Your child will learn that the school is supporting your efforts.

Sample Parent Resource Sheet: What to Do When Your Child Fails to Bring Home Assignments

Solving Homework Problems

What to Do When Your Child
Fails to Bring Home Assignments

When your child continually fails to bring home assigned homework, take action.

1. **State that you expect all homework assignments to be brought home.**
   Say, "I expect you to bring home all assigned work and all the books you need to complete it. If you finish your homework at school, I expect you to bring it home so that I can see it."

2. **Work with the teacher to make sure you know what homework has been assigned.**
   Students can use a weekly assignment sheet to record assignments. Ask the teacher to check and sign the sheet. When your child completes the assignments, you sign the sheet and have your child return it to the teacher.

3. **Provide praise and support when assignments are brought home.**
   Say, "It's great to see that you remembered to bring home all of your homework. I knew you could do it."

4. **Institute mandatory homework time.**
   If your child still fails to bring home assignments, institute mandatory homework time, which requires spending a specific amount of time on academic activities (reading, reviewing textbooks or class notes) whether homework is brought home or not. When students learn that they are expected to study in any case, they will be encouraged to bring home their assignments.

5. **Use a homework contract.**
   This motivator is a written, signed agreement between you and your child that states a reward or a point toward a prize will be earned for each day that homework is brought home and completed. (The younger the child, the more quickly the prize is earned.)

6. **Contact the teacher.**
   If the forgetfulness continues, discuss with the teacher the possibility of imposing loss of privileges at school. Your child will know that you and the school are working together to ensure responsible behavior.

Sample Parent Resource Sheet: What to Do When Your Child Takes All Night to Finish Homework

Solving Homework Problems

What to Do When Your Child Takes All Night to Finish Homework

Some children spend hours on homework when it's not necessary. They may stop and start and be easily distracted. In cases like this, here's what to do.

1. **Schedule daily homework time.**
   Allot a time each day when all other activities stop and your child must go to his study area and do homework. Say, "I expect you to get all of your homework done during this time. Your taking all evening to do it must stop."

2. **Make sure homework is done in a quiet area.**
   If your child has been working in a distracting environment, make sure there is no TV, stereo, or interruptions by siblings. If necessary, you may need to change the location of the study area.

3. **Give praise and support when homework is done on time.**
   Say, "I am really pleased to see that you got your homework done on time. I'm so proud of you."

4. **Give additional incentives when appropriate.**
   To help develop the habit of completing homework on time, play Beat the Clock. First determine how long homework should take. Then, at the start of homework time, set a timer. If homework is finished by the bell, a special privilege is earned.

5. **Back up your words with action.**
   Say, "You can either do your homework during daily homework time or lose these privileges during that time: You will not leave this house. You will not watch TV, listen to music, or use the telephone. You will sit here until all of your homework is done. The choice is yours." Stick to your demands. It may take your child several days to realize that you mean business.

Sample Parent Resource Sheet: What to Do When Your Child Will Not Do Homework on His Own

Solving Homework Problems

What to Do When Your Child Will Not Do Homework on His Own

If your child will not do homework without your assistance, first make sure that he is making a genuine effort to try to work alone. Follow these steps.

1. **State that you expect your child to work alone.**
   Say, "I expect you to do homework without my help. I will not sit with you or do your work for you, but I will be available for questions every so often."

2. **Schedule daily homework time.**
   Allot a time each day when all other activities stop and your child must go to his study area and do homework. Say, "I expect you to get all of your homework done during this time."

3. **Give praise and support when your child works independently.**
   When you see your child working alone, say, "I am really proud of the way you are doing all of this work on your own. I knew you could do it."

4. **Help your child build confidence.**
   If you think your child feels that homework is too much to handle on his own, "chunk" the assignments by breaking them down into smaller chunks that can be handled successfully.

5. **Offer help only after your child has genuinely tried to solve the problem independently.**
   There will be times when something is really too hard for your child to understand, but make sure that you don't step in until he has made a sincere effort to solve the problem at least twice.

6. **Back up your words with action.**
   If the problem persists, tell your child that at the end of homework time he must sit in his study area until the work is finished. Don't let tears, anger, or indifference manipulate you. Relying on you for help will only lead to greater dependence instead of the confidence you are trying to build.

Sample Parent Resource Sheet: What to Do When Your Child Waits Until the Last Minute to Finish Assignments

Solving Homework Problems

What to Do When Your Child Waits Until the Last Minute to Finish Assignments

If your child puts off starting long-range assignments and goes into a frenzy at the last minute, use the following suggestions.

1. **State that you expect long-range projects to be planned and completed responsibly.**
   Say, "I will not tolerate your putting off projects until just before they are due. This waiting until the last minute must stop."

2. **Ask the teacher for a long-range planner.**
   This planning sheet will help your child learn how to break down a large project into small, easily completed tasks over the period of time given for the project. Help your child fill in the steps on the planner.

3. **Give praise and support for your child as each step is completed.**
   Say, "You finished reading the book by the date you scheduled. Keep up the good work."

4. **Give additional motivators when appropriate.**
   If your child needs additional motivation to complete a project on time, institute a system that allows her to earn a point toward a reward or privilege each time a step is completed according to the schedule.

5. **Back up your words with action.**
   If the problem persists, impose restrictions. If your child fails to complete a step on the planner on time, take away a privilege (watching TV, using the phone) until the step is completed. Unless you set limits, your child is not going to believe that you mean business.

Sample Parent Resource Sheet: What to Do When Your Child Will Not Do Homework If You Aren't Home

Solving Homework Problems

What to Do When Your Child Will Not Do Homework If You Aren't Home

If your child will not do homework unless a parent is home, take these steps.

1. **State that you expect homework to be done whether you are home or not.**

2. **Schedule daily homework time.**
   Allot a time each day when all other activities stop and your child must go to his study area and do homework.

3. **Tell the person responsible for child care about daily homework time.**
   The caregiver should know when and where your child is expected to do homework.

4. **Monitor your child when you're not home to make sure homework is done.**
   Telephone your child, if possible, at the beginning and at the end of daily homework time to make sure the homework is getting done.

5. **Give praise and positive support.**
   Praise your child for work done in your absence. "You're doing a great job on homework when I am not here. Keep it up!"

6. **Use additional incentives, if necessary.**
   A homework contract can help your child develop the habit of doing homework without your supervision. It should state: that homework will be done whether you are home or not; the amount of time for completing homework; the number of points earned for completing homework; the reward earned when a certain number of points is attained.

7. **Back up your words with action.**
   Say, "You can do homework during daily homework time or you can choose not to have privileges. You will sit there until homework is finished." Make sure you follow through.

8. **Contact the teacher.**
   If the problem persists, discuss the possibility of imposing loss of privileges at school so that your child knows you and the teacher are working together to help your child behave responsibly.

Involving Parents in the Homework Process
REMINDERS

DO

➤ Let parents and students know exactly how you will deal with homework. Send home your homework policy before you give the first homework assignment.

➤ Give parents tips for helping their children do homework.

➤ Send home positive homework notes to parents.

➤ Assign a homework study buddy for each student.

➤ Let parents know about upcoming tests.

➤ Plan your homework when you plan your classroom lessons.

➤ Require students to write down all homework assignments in an assignment book or on an assignment sheet.

➤ Make sure that all your homework assignments are appropriate to the age and skill level of the student.

➤ Make sure that students understand how to do each homework assignment. Explain the assignment before students go home.

➤ Collect and comment on all homework. Students must know that you are paying attention to the work they do.

➤ Comment in a positive way on how each student did on an assignment, whenever possible.

(continued)

Involving Parents in the Homework Process
REMINDERS *(continued)*

DON'T

➤ Don't give last-minute, thrown-together homework assignments.

➤ Don't give homework assignments that have no objective.

➤ Don't give assignments that bear no connection to lessons.

➤ Don't expect students to know how to study unless they've been taught study skills.

➤ Don't overload students with homework. Be sensitive to the realities of their lives.

➤ Don't give only drill and practice homework.

Involving Parents in the Homework Process
CHECKLIST

Refer to this checklist as you plan your homework program.

Have you:

____ sent home a homework policy to all parents?

____ sent home homework and study skills tips to all parents?

____ planned to teach homework skills to your students?

____ set goals for yourself for sending home positive homework notes to parents?

____ set goals for yourself for sending home positive homework notes to students?

____ planned to assign family learning activities throughout the year?

Conducting Regularly Scheduled Parent Conferences

Successful parent conferences are an essential part of getting and keeping parent support. A regularly scheduled conference can be a pleasant, informative, and productive meeting for both parent and teacher—an opportunity to get to know one another and interact on behalf of the student.

A regularly scheduled conference isn't the time to surprise parents with negative information about their child's behavior or performance in school. These problems should never be saved for routine conferences. They need to be dealt with as soon as they occur.

This chapter covers two important areas to help you ensure that parent conferences are constructive and worthwhile for parent, student, and teacher:

- Prepare for the conference by planning exactly what you will do.

- Conduct the conference professionally and enthusiastically.

Prepare for the conference by planning exactly what you will do.

As with all parent contacts, planning makes the difference between a mediocre, lackluster meeting and a motivating, successful conference. The confidence you need to project at a conference is the result of careful planning. Follow each of the following steps and ensure a more productive conference for everyone.

Step 1: Send home a conference invitation.

Your invitation should be warm and friendly, but it must be informative as well. You will be supplying the parent with information *and* asking for some in return. This way, both of you will approach the conference better prepared and better informed.

Include the information that follows in your invitation.

Explain the purpose of having a parent conference.

Parents may not even know why they are being asked to come to a school conference. They may think that it's to hear bad news about their child, or that the conference is really a waste of their time. You need to let them know why you hold parent conferences and what you hope to accomplish. Stress the importance of the parent being there. Inform parents that you are holding conferences for the parents of all students.

Sample Parent Conference Note to Parents

> On November 11, 12, and 13, I will be holding conferences for the parents of all my students. This conference is a very important part of the school year. It is our opportunity to get to know each other better and to plan how we will work together for your child's benefit.

Offer parents flexible time choices.

A majority of parents work outside the home and can't always come to school in the middle of the day. It is extremely important that you recognize this fact and act accordingly. Few situations are as unsettling to a parent as feeling prevented from participating in their child's education.

Whenever possible, set up conference times early in the morning, late in the afternoon, in the evening, or even on weekends. If you feel that a parent may be more willing or able to attend a conference when it is held outside of school, suggest a public meeting place such as a coffee shop or a restaurant. It may not be as convenient for you, but parents will appreciate your willingness to recognize the realities of their lives. No matter when and where you hold the conference, make sure it is conducted in a professional manner.

Give parents as much choice as possible in choosing the day of the week and the time for the conference. Your invitation might include a portion that is returned to you indicating when the parent can attend. (Suggestion: Some teachers circulate a parent-conference-time schedule at Back-to-School Night. The schedule lists all dates and times available for conferences. Parents sign their names next to the dates and times desired. As conference time approaches, reminders are sent home to parents.)

Ask parents to let you know what they would like to discuss.

Include a section on the invitation for the parent to list any issues he would like to discuss at the conference. This gives a parent the opportunity to think in advance about what he would like to talk about. And having this information ahead of time will better prepare you to address the parent's concerns.

Write a personal comment on the invitation.

Whenever you personalize a reproduced letter that goes home, you are showing parents that you've put in just a bit more effort and care. Take a minute or two to jot down a friendly line, such as "I'm looking forward to talking with you," on the parent conference invitation. And be sure to sign your name. Parents will notice these personal touches.

Step 2: Plan the physical environment.

It's difficult to feel professional (or to be perceived as such) when you are sitting face-to-face with a parent who is stuffed behind a primary desk or perched precariously on an undersized chair. Make sure parents are comfortable during the conference. Arrange to have adult-sized chairs in your room.

If possible, set up a coffee maker and offer coffee and/or tea. Make a positive impression before the conference begins by giving some thought to the comfort of parents as they wait their turn. Place two chairs outside the door, along with a stack of student textbooks and workbooks for parents to look at.

Step 3: Put together samples of each student's class work.

Have examples of the student's class work available for the conference. This will demonstrate that you took considerable time and thought to prepare for the meeting about this specific student. It communicates not only that you take your job seriously, but also that you genuinely care about this particular student. Throughout the conference, use the work to help you illustrate statements you are making to the parents regarding the student's performance in the classroom.

Sample Parent Conference Invitation

Dear Parent(s)

During the week of November 14 to 18 I will be holding conferences with the parents of all my students. I am looking forward to this opportunity for us to talk about your child's educational experiences this year. At the conference we will discuss your child's progress in school, my goals for the remainder of the year, and any other issues that affect you or your child. I am certain that this meeting will be productive for all of us! Working together, we can make this the best year ever for your child.

Sincerely,

Mr. Chung

Please take a few moments to fill out the lower portion of this letter. When completed, send it back to school.

- -

Parent's name _____

Student's name _____

Please check off your first and second choices of the dates and times most convenient for you. I will do my best to set our meeting for your first-choice time.

These are the dates I prefer:

____ Monday, November 14   ____ Thursday, November 17
____ Tuesday, November 15   ____ Friday, November 18
____ Wednesday, November 16

These are the times I prefer:

____ Morning   ____ Afternoon   ____ Evening

If you have concerns or questions you'd like to discuss with me at the conference, please write them down below. I would like to take that opportunity to talk about the issues that are important to you.

_____

_____

_____

_____

Step 4: Fill out a Parent Conference Planning and Note Sheet for each student before meeting the parent(s).

A parent conference must be tightly structured. You have only a limited amount of time, and much to discuss. Prepare yourself by noting all the issues you wish to discuss. Knowing in advance what you are going to talk about can save you from inadvertently leaving out important points. If you are prepared, you'll be more relaxed. And when you are relaxed, your confidence will show and the parent will, in turn, feel more confidence in you.

Use the Parent Conference Planning and Note Sheet on page 118 to structure your conferences. Each of the points listed should be addressed when you meet with parents. Notice that three of the points are to be filled in with parent comments during the conference.

Here is a detailed look at each point listed on the planning sheet and how it would be approached in the conference.

1. **Begin by sharing an example of the unique qualities of the child.**

   Parents come to conferences to learn about their child's progress. They also want to be satisfied that the teacher knows about, understands, and appreciates the unique qualities of their child. It is important for you to show parents that you've taken the time and interest to get to know their child. For example:

   "Kara has a real passion for art. It is a pleasure to watch her when she is involved in painting."

   "Maureen is a leader among her classmates. Let me tell you how she handled a tough situation between several students."

2. **Give an update on any past problems the student had.**

   If you have dealt with the parent about a problem in the past, make sure you spend some time updating the current status of the situation. It's important to attend to this as soon as possible because the parent will most likely be anxious about it, and that anxiety may keep him from listening to anything else.

   "I'm happy to tell you that Erin is turning in all of her homework assignments now."

   "Felipe is doing much better controlling his temper. I can see the effort he's making."

   "Math continues to be a problem for Taylor, but during this conference we're going to discuss what can be done to help him at home."

Sample Parent Conference Planning and Note Sheet

Parent Conference Planning and Note Sheet

Student's Name _____ Time _____

Parent's Name _____ Date _____

1. Example of student's unique quality:

   _____

2. Past problems of the student to be updated at the conference:

   _____

3. Academic strengths of the student:

   _____

4. Academic weaknesses of the student that should be discussed:

   _____

5. Parent input on student's academic performance:

   _____

6. Academic goals for the student for the rest of the year:

   _____

7. Social strengths of the student:

   _____

8. Any weaknesses in the area of social development the student has:

   _____

9. Social development goals for the student for the rest of the year:

   _____

10. Parent input regarding student's social behavior:

    _____

11. Additional issues parent wishes to discuss:

    _____

3. **Discuss academic strengths of the student.**
   Focus on the positive academic strengths of the student. Show examples of class work at this time. If appropriate, you may wish to use the student's report card as a guide for this discussion.

   "Here's where Jaime was at the start of the year in reading. Now look at this. He's moved ahead three levels. You can see from these tests that his comprehension skills are excellent."

   "Troy did a great job organizing and writing this term paper. His research was thorough, his note cards well written, and the final paper was carefully thought out and interesting to read."

4. **If appropriate, discuss academic weaknesses of the student.**
   If the child is having academic problems, let the parent know you are taking steps to improve the situation.

   "I'm aware, of course, that Kenneth is struggling to keep up in Spanish. I have some lessons on tape that I think will help him. I'd like to send them home with you. Here's how to use them . . ."

   "Algebra One is very difficult for Brittany. I've arranged to have her work with a senior tutor two days a week during class time."

5. **Get parental input on the student's academic performance.**
   Ask parents how they feel their child is doing in school. It is important that parents have the opportunity to give feedback. If they feel that there's a problem you are overlooking, you need to address the issue and clear up any misunderstanding. Ask questions such as:

   "Are you satisfied with your child's academic performance?"

   "Do you have any concerns about how your child is doing in school?"

   Take notes on what the parents say, and make sure parents know that you find their input important and valuable. Let them know that, if appropriate, you are prepared to adjust your dealings with their child accordingly.

6. **Discuss academic goals for the student for the remainder of the year.**
   Talk to the parent about what you'd like to see the child accomplish the rest of the year. Get the parent's input, too. Knowing that both of you have the same goals will help establish a rapport that may be needed if difficulties arise later.

"I would like to see Jonelle reading at grade level by June. Considering how well she's doing now, I think we will meet this goal. What goals would you like to see Jonelle achieve?"

"Rebecca's research skills should improve considerably over the next few months. We will be doing some assignments geared toward this goal. How do you see Rebecca's progress? Do you have any suggestions?"

7. Present the social strengths of the student.

Discuss the student's social behavior in your class by focusing on his strengths in relating to peers. Be prepared to give specific examples.

"Larry is always there to help out a friend. His loyalty is really valued by the other students. They know they can count on him."

"Raffi's exuberance and spirit make him someone that students and teachers enjoy being with."

8. If appropriate, discuss the student's weaknesses in social interactions.

Be sensitive. Link any suggestions or observations you have to a positive statement or observation.

"I'd like to see Ben feel more confident about himself when he's in a group. He's a smart boy, but I'm not so sure he thinks so."

"As you are aware, Paula too often lets anger control her. I think, however, that the behavior contract you are using at home and I'm using at school is making a difference."

9. Discuss your goals for the student, in the area of social development, for the remainder of the school year.

"I would like to see Kathryn become a bit more assertive in class. I know she has opinions she'd like to offer, but she holds back. I'm going to have the students do some cooperative learning activities. The small-group setting should help Kathryn overcome some of her hesitance."

10. Get parental input regarding the student's social behavior.

Ask the parent how she perceives the child is doing socially. Make sure you open the door to a discussion of the parent's suggestions for improving the situation.

"Do you feel that your child is happy in school?"

"What are your concerns regarding your child's relationships with other students?"

"How do you think we could help Yuki feel more confident about herself?"

11. **Finally, talk about any other issues parents may wish to discuss.**
Ask if there's anything else the parent would like to talk about with you. At this time, you should also address any issues that the parent wrote about on the conference notification.

Conduct the conference professionally and enthusiastically.

Set a professional, caring tone.

The attitude you project at the conference is what will ultimately win a parent's confidence, trust, and support. Keep the "golden rule" of parent communication in mind at all times: Treat parents the way you would want to be treated. At a conference, the parent is your guest in the classroom. You are the host and it's your responsibility to see that it is a pleasurable, productive, and informative experience.

Greet the parent warmly.

First impressions do count. Whether it's 6:30 in the morning or 7:30 at night, wake up, put on a smile, and make the parent feel welcome. Greet the parent at the door and give a firm handshake before sitting down. Offer coffee or tea and spend a moment or two putting the parent at ease.

Refer to your planning sheet as you proceed through the conference.

Your planning sheet helped you focus on your goals as you planned for the meeting. Be sure you use this valuable resource during the conference, too. Keep it in front of you as you speak, and jot down points of interest as they come up.

Use effective listening and communication skills.

The way you speak and listen to a parent can have great impact in enhancing that parent's trust and confidence in what you are saying. Your body language carries part of your message.

Make sure that your words and your actions communicate that you are an open and caring teacher, here to help your students succeed. Be sensitive to the parent, treating him the way you would want to be treated if your own child were the object of the conversation. With this in mind, be on the lookout for any roadblocks that may appear, and use your communication skills to move the parent past the roadblock.

This conference is a good opportunity for you to interact with parents in a positive, supportive atmosphere. Make the most of it. Don't ignore a parent's feelings of stress, hostility, or confusion. Take these feelings seriously and address them openly. Your confident, professional attitude and appropriate responses can turn an uninvolved parent into a supportive one.

In Chapter 9, we will discuss effective communication skills that will help you succeed in your interactions with parents.

Close the conference on a positive, optimistic note.

At the close of the conference, rise, shake the parent's hand, and walk together to the door. Make sure your parting comments are sincere. Leave the parent with a positive, confident feeling that you are an educator who really cares, and who will be there for the child all year long.

> "I'm so glad we've had this conference, Mrs. Peterson. I think the goals we both have for your son are clear. And now that we know each other better, I'm sure we can work together to make this year a real success for Rob. I look forward to speaking to you again soon."

Conducting Regularly Scheduled
Parent Conferences
REMINDERS

DO

➤ Arrive at the conference site before the parent.

➤ Greet the parent warmly.

➤ Usher the parent to the seat you've selected.

➤ Look the parent in the eyes when speaking.

➤ Address the parent often by name.

➤ Say something complimentary about the student early in the conference.

➤ Hand the parent the child's work to look over. Point out examples of work that should be noted.

➤ Have study or academic tips available to give to parents.

➤ Ask the parent for his input regarding the student.

➤ End the conference on time, and schedule another one if needed.

➤ Make detailed notes of what was discussed.

DON'T

➤ Don't surprise parents with new problems. Parents should be notified the moment a problem arises.

➤ Don't make small talk. Use every moment of the parent's time to discuss the student's progress.

➤ Don't discuss other students, even if the parent tries to.

➤ Don't do all the talking. You want to maintain control of the conference, but you should allow the parent time to discuss his concerns and ideas. You may learn something important that can help you in dealing with the child.

Conducting Regularly Scheduled
Parent Conferences
CHECKLIST

Refer to this checklist when you plan your parent-teacher conferences.

Have you:

____ sent an invitation that explains why parents should attend the conference?

____ made flexible time choices available to parents?

____ asked parents to let you know what they would like to discuss?

____ organized samples of each student's class work?

____ planned where parents will sit for the conference?

____ arranged for coffee or tea?

____ filled out a Parent Conference Form for each student?

____ collected appropriate study or academic tips to give parents so that they can help their child at home?

Demonstrating Sensitivity and Awareness

The key to parent involvement is communication. The key to successful communication is sensitivity and awareness. This chapter addresses two important ways to boost your skills:

- Practice sensitivity in your interactions with parents.

- Show that you are aware of a family's special situation.

Practice sensitivity in your interactions with parents.

Successful communication depends on more than what you are prepared to say. It also depends on how you listen and react to what a parent says. You can't anticipate a parent's words, but the following techniques will help you show parents that you are sensitive to their feelings and are prepared to adjust your own behavior accordingly.

Be aware of your body language and tone of voice.

Body language and tone of voice carry an important part of your message. Therefore, it is very important that you are aware of and adjust these communication tools to convey caring, accessibility, openness, and warmth.

- When meeting with a parent face-to-face, lean forward slightly while he is speaking. This shows that you are interested in what is being said.

- Maintain eye contact. Do not cross your arms. Instead, show openness and a willingness to listen.

■ Make sure there are no physical barriers between you and the parent. It's best to sit next to each other at a table. Don't sit at your desk with the parent on the other side. The seating arrangement has to reflect that you accept the parent as an equal partner in her child's education.

■ In all conversations with parents, your tone of voice should show your confidence and calmness. Make sure that irritation, frustration, or annoyance doesn't creep into your manner of speech. Don't raise your voice, and remain calm and polite at all times. Speak to every parent the way you'd like to be spoken to.

■ In all conversations with parents, you must be willing to listen to what the parent has to say. Don't take over the conversation. Don't interrupt. Feel free to add some verbal assurances ("I understand," etc.) to show that you are listening.

Use the reflective listening technique.

It is important, especially if a parent is upset, that you convey your empathy with what he is saying. A technique called reflective listening is very effective to show that you are sensitive to a parent's situation. When you use this technique, you simply reflect back in words that you heard what the parent said and understand how he feels. You are not making a judgment about what is being said. You are not agreeing or disagreeing. You are simply letting the parent know that you hear and you understand. This is a powerful technique that will demonstrate to a parent that you respect the feelings he is expressing.

Preface your reflective response with comments such as "I hear how upset you are," or "I understand how upset you are about all of this."

Here are some sample comments from parents, with the teacher's reflective response.

Parent: I don't know what to do with that boy. He just won't listen to me.

Teacher: *(Reflective response)* I hear how upset you are about your son.

Parent: I honestly believe his problems are caused by other children.

Teacher: *(Reflective response)* I hear what you are saying.

Parent:	You need to understand that I'm a single mom. I work. I don't have any time to deal with this.
Teacher:	*(Reflective response)* I understand how overwhelmed you must feel.
Parent:	I fight every night with him to try to get him to do his homework.
Teacher:	*(Reflective response)* I hear how frustrated you are.
Parent:	I really don't know if she should be held back.
Teacher:	*(Reflective response)* I understand what a difficult choice that must be.

Reflective listening is a valuable skill. Combined with an awareness of your body language, it can greatly increase your ability to communicate with parents.

Use a translator when necessary.

When dealing with parents from a different cultural or linguistic background, you may need to use the services of a translator. Here are a few important guidelines to keep in mind:

- Sit facing the parent, with the translator seated next to you.

- As you speak, always look directly at the parent, never at the translator. When the translator speaks, continue to look at the parent.

- Keep your eyes on the parent when he speaks, not on the translator. Continue to do so when the translator speaks.

In other words, make sure that the conference is between you and the parent, not between you, the parent, and the translator. Pay attention to your body language. Lean forward as you speak. Maintain eye contact and, through your gestures and attitude, exude warmth and caring that will transcend spoken words in any culture.

Show that you are aware of a family's special situation.

Today, a teacher can't assume that one method or style of communication will fit the needs of all. Teachers work with many kinds of families, including stepfamilies, single-parent and two-parent families, same-sex parents, families torn by poverty or wrestling with divorce, two-income families, transient families, non–English-speaking families, and families of various ethnic or cultural backgrounds. An effective teacher must at all times be aware of the varying realities of the families of his students.

Throughout *Parents on Your Side,* you are given a wide variety of suggestions to guide you in your communications with parents. Before you put any of these ideas to use, take time to think about the person with whom you will be communicating. Make every effort to satisfy yourself that you are, to the best of your ability, communicating in an appropriate manner.

Take special care to be aware of the cultural diversity of your students and to gain an understanding of their varying cultural expectations and values. Let that knowledge guide your words and actions throughout the year. Acceptable behaviors or manners in one culture may not be the same in another.

Your professional judgment must lead you as you communicate with every parent. Yet it is always appropriate to practice sensitivity and show awareness toward a parent's specific situation, particularly if it is different from your own. Your behavior is guided by your own values, beliefs, and expectations, as is the behavior of your students' parents. Let your attitude and behavior show that you accept the parents' background and are willing to work with them to help their children succeed in school.

Demonstrating Sensitivity and Awareness
REMINDERS

DO

➤ Be aware of your body language and tone of voice in all of your communications with parents.

➤ Communicate confidence and calmness at all times, and demonstrate openness and genuine interest in what a parent has to say.

➤ Practice reflective listening to show you empathize with a parent's situation.

➤ Educate yourself about appropriate ways to communicate with parents from different social and cultural backgrounds.

DON'T

➤ Don't treat every parent alike. Make every effort to adjust your behavior and attitude to suit the individual with whom you are dealing.

➤ Don't allow your preconceptions about a parent's background to come between you and an open dialogue with the parent.

➤ Don't dominate a conversation.

➤ Don't interrupt.

➤ Don't let irritation, frustration, or anger affect your tone of voice, body language, or attitude toward a parent.

Demonstrating Sensitivity and Awareness CHECKLIST

Refer to this checklist as you plan your communication with parents.

Have you:

____ educated yourself about the expectations, behaviors, and values guiding the particular parent with whom you are meeting?

____ honestly evaluated your own preconceptions about the parent's specific background?

____ reviewed the tips on body language and reflective listening?

____ prepared the meeting room to communicate that you consider the parent a partner in the child's education?

THREE

How to Work With
Parents to Solve Problems

Successful communication with parents often includes involving parents in solving a student's behavior or academic problem. This section of *Parents on Your Side* will offer practical advice on how to enlist parent support in problematic situations.

Chapter 10: Documenting Problems

In order to be able to communicate with parents effectively about a problem with their child, it is essential that you have sufficient information about problems as they appear. This chapter will give some suggestions on how to keep a record of student behavior and performance.

Chapter 11: Contacting Parents at the First Sign of a Problem

In this chapter, you will learn how to contact parents when problems arise. Contact them as soon as possible in order to avoid the problem getting worse.

Chapter 12: Conducting a Problem-Solving Conference

If a student's behavior or performance does not improve, it may be necessary to conduct a problem-solving conference with the parent. This chapter will offer advice on how to prepare for and conduct such a conference so that it is most effective.

Chapter 13: Using a Home-School Contract

This chapter will show you how to prepare and manage a contract between you, the parent, and the student to improve the student's behavior. The contract stipulates the desired student behavior, the teacher's disciplinary measures administered in case of problems, and the parent's follow-through at home.

Chapter 14: Providing Support for Parents' Disciplinary Efforts

This chapter offers suggestions for you to pass on to parents who need your help in dealing with their children's behavior or academic problems. These suggestions comprise disciplinary techniques and ideas to help parents reach out to their children.

Chapter 15: Dealing with Difficult Situations

In your career, you will encounter difficult parents. This chapter will offer general strategies for dealing with a parent's angry criticism and for reaching even the most reluctant parent.

Documenting Problems

When it comes to their child's poor performance, parents often resist believing what they are told. Nobody likes to hear bad news. It's especially hard for parents to hear anything negative about their child. They may feel it reflects on their parenting abilities or feel that it's something they have no control over. They may take the bad news personally and may resist your efforts to improve the situation.

Therefore, it will benefit both you and the parents to keep accurate documentation of all academic or behavioral problems as they occur. Documentation will strengthen your position as a professional, help you communicate clearly to parents, and provide strong evidence to parents who may question your word.

Early in the school year, your experience and intuition will guide you in recognizing those students who may have problems. It is vital that you begin documenting their actions immediately. Having anecdotal records will be necessary when you seek the support of administrators and parents.

This chapter addresses the following ways to use documentation in your efforts to change a problem into a solution:

- Document situations in a nonjudgmental manner.

- Choose a record-keeping system.

- Use your documentation.

Document situations in a nonjudgmental manner.

Detailed record keeping of the situation is not meant as an excuse to try and find fault with a particular student. Rather than labeling a student as incorrigible, make sure to document an unbiased account of what the student did and what you did to help the student correct the behavior.

A nonjudgmental record of the situation will enable you to remain fair and impartial when meeting with parents and administrators.

Be specific in your description of the problem.

When you write your documentation, keep away from vague opinions.

"Sean misbehaved all day long."

"Kerry didn't do anything she was supposed to do today."

Base your statements on factual, observable data.

"Yesterday, Sean threw his lunch tray on the ground and shoved other children in three separate instances."

"Today during reading, Louise repeatedly jumped up and bothered her neighbor."

Consistent, specific documentation will enable you to give a nonjudgmental account of a student's performance. Documentation enables you to tell parents exactly what's going on—behaviorally, academically, or with homework.

Choose a record-keeping system.

Use any of the following methods for documenting student performance:

- A small notebook or computer file with one page designated for each student. Insert a page for the student only when the first infraction occurs. Secondary teachers usually designate a documentation section for each class period.

- $3\frac{1}{2} \times 5\frac{1}{2}$ inch index cards, alphabetically arranged in a file box, one for each student.

- A loose-leaf notebook with one or more pages per student. (This is especially useful for a class with many difficult students.)

An anecdotal record should include the following information:

- Student's name and class

- Date, time, and place of incident
- Description of problem
- Action taken

Sample Documentation on 3½ × 5½ Inch Index Card

> **Johnson, Kim   Period 4**
>
> 10/8   Kim cut math class. Phoned Mr. Johnson. Said he won't let her go out with friends if it happens again.
>
> 10/20   Kim cut class. Sent note to Mr. Johnson.
>
> 10/24   Kim cut class. Sent note to Mr. Johnson to arrange a conference. No response as of 10/26.
>
> 10/30   Called Mr. Johnson. Left message to return call. No response.
>
> 11/20   Principal sent note to arrange conference.

Sample Documentation in Small Notebook or Computer File

Lois Simon   Grade 4

Date/Time	Place	Rule Broken	Action Taken
9/15 10:45	Classroom	Refused to return to seat	Reminder
9/15 1:20	Classroom	Running in class	Lose 10 minutes recess
9/15 1:40	Classroom	Called out without raising hand	Lose 20 minutes recess
9/18 2:00	Hallway	Ran out of line for drink of water	Reminder
9/18 2:40	Gym	Continued playing after whistle blew	No gym next week

Organize and file your documentation.

Create a separate folder for each student with behavioral or academic problems. Include the following information in each folder:

- Student's name and class

- Home phone number

- Work phone number(s)

- Emergency phone number

Keep your anecdotal record in the file.

In addition, keep copies of all correspondence you have had with parents regarding the student's problem(s). Make notes during phone calls and write down any agreements reached between you and the parent. Make copies of any letters or notes that you have sent to parents as well as copies of all notes and letters received from them. Don't leave anything to memory.

Maintain your records so that you will have a complete chronological history of the student's problem(s). Later, when you need to refer to them or show them to an administrator or parent, a complete and accurate timeline of events will enable you to present the problem clearly and professionally. Confidence comes from knowing you've done everything possible to solve a student's problem and from having the records to prove it.

You may need to tape-record your class.

If you are dealing with a particularly difficult situation—if you feel that a parent may not trust you, or if a parent believes you are the cause of the problem—it may be useful to tape-record your class so the parents can hear exactly how their child behaves.

There are two ways to do this with two distinctly different outcomes.

- Do not tell the student you will be recording the class. This method allows parents to actually witness their child's problem behavior.

- Tell the student ahead of time that you will be recording the class. Often mentioning that you will be tape-recording the class may be enough to improve the student's behavior. This in itself may be a solution to the problem, and you may never have to play the recording for the parents.

Use your documentation.

Have documentation records with you when you meet with parents. This will make sure that

- parents can read the specific behaviors their child engaged in;

- no one can question how you handled the situation;

- your word cannot be pitted against that of a student;

- you and the student's parents can address specific problems directly and find solutions.

In severe cases, the anecdotal record will show that the student has been given due process and will justify the following:

- Intervention of the principal

- Removal of the child from your class to be placed in another class

- Referral to a counselor or therapist

- Suspension

- Removal from school

- Special education placement

REMEMBER: Having specific records of a student's problems will enable you to hold a more effective problem-solving conference. You will feel confident knowing you did everything you could to deal with the problem yourself. You will not be flustered and will not have to rely on your memory.

Documenting Problems
REMINDERS

DO

➤ Begin documenting problems as soon as they appear.

➤ Make sure your documentation relates factual, observable data.

➤ Use your documentation when you seek support from an administrator or parents.

➤ Use the documentation to help you pinpoint specific problems a student is having.

➤ Include the time, place, and details of the incident, and the names of those involved.

➤ Organize your files chronologically so that you can present a clear, accurate picture of the history of the problem.

DON'T

➤ Don't use documenting a student's problem behavior to find fault with him.

➤ Don't include your own opinions in your documentation.

➤ Don't let your documentation lapse. To be effective, you must keep consistent, up-to-date records.

Documenting Problems
CHECKLIST

Refer to this checklist as you begin to document student problems.

Have you:

____ begun documenting problems as soon as they appear?

____ based your documentation on factual, observable data?

____ avoided writing down vague opinions?

____ created a documentation file for each student as the need arises?

____ included all pertinent communication and notes in the file?

____ organized your documentation chronologically?

Contacting Parents at the First Sign of a Problem

A common complaint among parents is that teachers wait too long before contacting them about a problem. It doesn't matter whether it's the first week of school or even the first day. As soon as you become aware of an academic or behavioral problem that parents should know about, contact them. This issue is at the core of any parental involvement plan. Parents can't be expected to get involved if they don't know what's going on.

In this chapter, the following topics will help you make the decision to call parents and follow through successfully:

- When should you contact a parent?

- The best way to contact parents is by phone.

- Make sure you contact hard-to-reach parents.

- Follow up on the initial contact.

- File your notes and records.

When should you contact a parent?

How do you know when you should contact a parent about a problem? Many situations are very clear: severe fighting, extreme emotional distress, a student who refuses to work or turn in homework, or a student who cannot do the work. You don't think twice about involving parents when these situations occur. But what about the day-to-day instances that may not be so obvious? In most cases, your own good judgment will be your best guide.

If you are uncertain about contacting a parent, again use the "your own child" test. This test will put you in the position of the parent and help clarify whether or not parental help is called for.

Follow these steps:

1. Assume that you have a child of your own who is the same age as the student in question.

2. If your child had the same problem in school as that student, would you want to be called?

3. If the answer is yes, call the parent. If the answer is no, do not call the parent.

For example, if your own child forgot to bring her book to class one day, would you want to be called? Most likely the answer is no. If, on the other hand, your own child forgot her book three days in a row, you most likely would want to know. The "your own child" test will help to focus your attention on problems that need parental involvement, and it will guide you to treat parents the way you would want to be treated.

You will find that by using this test you will increase your contact with parents. And increasing contact with parents will increase the probability of parent support.

The best way to contact parents is by phone.

Once you've decided that you are going to contact a parent, how are you going to get in touch? A phone call is unquestionably the best way to contact parents when there is an issue that needs prompt attention. It's personal, it's immediate, and it gives you the opportunity to clearly explain the situation and answer right away any questions the parent may have.

Calling parents should not make you nervous or hesitant. You know that you are making the call in the best interests of your student. You have every right and obligation to involve the parent if you think the situation calls for it. Relax. You can conduct a productive call. Planning is the key. You'll find that you can handle any call if you know in advance what you are going to say.

Write down what you will say.

Remember that before you pick up the phone, you need to outline what you are going to say to the parent. These notes will be your script for conducting the call, and the writing process will help you think through and clarify the points you want to make. Having the notes in front of you while you're speaking will keep you from getting nervous and forgetting important details.

Plan to address each of the points listed on the sample planning sheet below. Fill out a sheet like this each time you prepare for a problem-solving phone call.

Sample Parent Phone Call Worksheet

Parent Phone Call Worksheet
Initial Phone Call About a Problem

Teacher _____ Grade _____

Student's Name _____

Name of Parent(s) or Guardian _____

Phone number(s) _____

Date of call _____

Brief description of problem: _____
_____

Write down important points you will cover with parents.

1. Begin with a statement of concern.

2. Describe the specific behavior that necessitated the call.

3. Describe the steps you have taken to solve the problem.

4. Get parental input.

5. Present your solutions to the problem (what you will do; what you want the parent to do).

6. Express confidence in your ability to solve the problem.

7. Inform parents that you will follow up with them.

Notes: _____
_____
_____

By addressing these points, you will find that your phone conversation will be both informative and effective. Let's take a closer look.

1. **Begin with a statement of concern.**

   Your introductory statement will set the tone for the entire conversation. Remember that even though you're calling about a problem, you can still project a positive, supportive, and sensitive attitude. Keep in mind that you're not calling to place blame or complain. You're calling because you care about the student. Through your words, let the parent know that the welfare of his child is your utmost concern. When a parent hears concern rather than an accusation, he will be much more receptive to you.

   The following examples illustrate this point.

   "Mrs. Grozny, I'm calling because

   ➤ I'm concerned about how little work Theo is doing."

   ➤ I'm concerned that Linda does not get along with the other students."

   Notice that the statements express concern for the student and outline the problem in a more positive way that invites further dialogue.

2. **Describe the specific behavior that necessitated the call.**

   Tell the parent in specific, observable terms what the child did or did not do. An observable behavior is behavior you can watch going on, such as talking out, not turning in assignments, refusing to follow directions, or hitting a classmate. Always mention the specific behavior and the number of times the problem has occurred.

   "The reason I'm concerned is

   ➤ Seth shouted out in class four times today."

   ➤ Lorenzo has refused to do any of his work in class for two days now."

   ➤ Nicole had two fights today with other students."

   These specific statements about observable behavior tell the parents exactly what happened. Avoid making vague statements that do not clearly communicate the problem.

   "He's having problems again."

   "She's just not behaving."

Comments such as these don't give parents any real information at all. In fact, they may give the parent the impression that you don't like and are picking on the child. Uninformative, negative comments will only serve to make parents defensive.

In addition, avoid making negative, judgmental comments such as:

"The reason I'm calling is

➤   your child has a bad attitude."

➤   your child is mean to other students."

➤   your child is lazy."

Again, statements such as these give no valid information and will immediately alienate a parent.

3. **Describe the steps you have taken to solve the problem.**
    It's important that parents recognize that you have already taken appropriate action to deal with the situation—that you're not calling them in lieu of attempting to solve the problem yourself. Be specific. Tell them exactly what you have done.

    "I discussed your child's behavior with him and reviewed the rules of our classroom discipline plan. He understands the corrective actions for not following them, and, accordingly, twice he has been last to go to recess. I have also made a point of giving him extra positive attention when he is behaving."

    "When Lynne refused to do her work in class, I had her stay in my room during lunch to complete the assignment. In addition, I have spoken with her on three occasions regarding how she needs to complete her assignments. To further encourage her, I've been giving her a point whenever she does her work. When she earns five points, she can have extra free time."

    "I had a conference with your son about his fighting. He was sent to the principal's office when he continued to fight, and the principal and I had a conference regarding how to help him."

4. **Get parental input.**
    Ask the parent if there's anything she can add that might help solve the problem. The parent may have unique insights into the student's personality, and may know why the student continues to have a problem and how to help him

move beyond it. Listen carefully to what the parent has to say, and be prepared to take suggestions into account.

"Is there anything you can tell me that might help us solve this problem?"

5. **Present your solutions to the problem.**
    Be prepared to tell the parent exactly what you are going to do, and what you would like the parent to do. Don't dispense parenting advice. It is not your place to change a parent's child-rearing methods. It is your place, however, to ask a parent for her support in your efforts to educate the child. In an initial phone call about a problem, the most important thing you can ask the parent to do is let the child know that you called and that you and the parent both are concerned about the problem.

    "Here's what I will do at school: I'll continue to give Gary plenty of positive support when he does turn in homework on time. When he doesn't, he will have to complete it during detention. Would you tell Gary I called, and that I am concerned that he isn't turning in his homework? Tell him that you are concerned also. I want Gary to know that both of us are working together to help him do better in school."

6. **Express confidence in your ability to solve the problem.**
    Whenever there is a problem, parents may become anxious. They need to know that they are dealing with a skilled teacher who has the confidence and the ability to work with their child to eliminate the problem. Keep the pediatrician analogy in mind. When a child is ill, a parent wants to hear the doctor say, "Don't worry. I know how to solve the problem. It will be taken care of." The last thing a parent wants to hear is, "I don't know how to handle this, but I'll do my best." Let parents know that you know what to do. Emphasize that with the parents' support you know you will get results. Your tone and attitude during this conversation should help express your confidence.
    Make statements such as:

    "Mr. Hill, I've worked with many children like Tom. Don't worry. Together we will help him."

    "Mrs. Jacobs, I've had a lot of experience with young people who have the same problem as Tamar. I know that by working together we will get results!"

    "Mrs. Rivera, it's going to be just fine. Don't worry. I know how to motivate children like Carlos, and I know that together we will get results."

7. **Inform parents that you will follow up with them.**

   When you tell parents that you will follow up on this conversation, you are promising that something is going to happen, that the problem is not going to be swept under the rug. Follow-up contact is vital if parents are going to believe in your commitment. It is also vital for positioning yourself to enlist their support in the future. Before ending the conversation, tell parents when they can expect to hear from you again.

   "I will contact you in two days and let you know how things are going with Tamar."

   "I'll call you tomorrow and tell you about David's success!"

Be sensitive and alert.

Your phone call should not be a one-sided conversation. You are building a foundation for future cooperative efforts with the parent. Be sure to ask for parental input at comfortable, appropriate intervals. Don't push parents, but open the door for them to add any insights they may have. If and when they do, make sure you take the time to really listen to any concerns they may express.

Parents know and care about their children, and even though they may not have been able to get a handle on the particular problem you are contacting them about, they may offer insights that are extremely valuable to your efforts.

Take parents seriously: don't discount their comments, and always show your willingness to listen and learn. Put yourself in the parent's position and approach him in the manner you would like to be approached. Listen for any roadblocks that might appear and help the parent move past them.

Sample Initial Phone Call About a Problem

Below is a conversation that incorporates all of the points discussed. Notice that while asking the parent for cooperation, the teacher not only gives the parent specific information but also shows plenty of professional confidence.

The teacher begins with a statement of concern and then describes the specific behavior that necessitated the call.

"Mr. Jonas, this is Judy Spelling, Sandra's teacher. I'm calling because I'm concerned that Sandra has not been turning in her homework assignments. Last week, she didn't turn in three math assignments and two social studies exercises. Today, I did not receive another math assignment."

Now the teacher describes the steps she has already taken to solve the problem.

"I have discussed this situation with Sandra and reviewed the homework rules with her. She knows that her report card grade will drop if she keeps missing homework. Can you think of anything that might help us solve this problem?"

The teacher asks for parental input. She listens carefully to the response and shows her willingness to possibly adapt her own strategies to the parent's suggestions.

The teacher then presents her solutions to the problem.

"Mr. Jonas, I'd like us to work together to help Sandra develop better homework habits. Here's what I'd like to do: I am going to attach a slip to each assignment that goes home. Please ask to see all of her assignments each night. When she has finished the work, sign the slip. Chances are, your checking the work will be enough to motivate Sandra, but I'll also add a little extra incentive here at school. Each time I receive a completed assignment on time, Sandra will receive a point. When she earns 10 points I will reward her with extra time in the library, which she does enjoy."

The teacher expresses confidence that the problem can be solved.

"Mr. Jonas, I'm certain that by working together we can help Sandra do a better job at school. She's a bright girl with a lot of potential. Please tell Sandra I called you and that I am concerned about this problem. Let her know that you are concerned about it, too."

Follow-up contact is arranged and the conversation concludes on an enthusiastic, upbeat note.

"I am going to call you next Monday and let you know how everything is working out. I'm sure I'll be calling with good news! In the meantime, be sure to give Sandra plenty of praise when she does her homework. Believe me, it makes a difference.

"I'm glad we've had this opportunity to talk. I look forward to our next conversation."

Make sure you contact hard-to-reach parents.

Don't give up trying to contact a parent just because you've dialed home twice and not received an answer. You have to make every effort to reach a parent. You wouldn't accept defeat if the child were physically ill and needed her parents.

Somehow you'd find a way to get through. Keep in mind that a problem ignored will probably get worse, and then parents will wonder why they weren't informed earlier. Remember that it is your responsibility to make all possible effort to contact a parent.

Here are some additional strategies you can use.

Send a letter.

If you cannot reach a parent by phone, a letter home is your next option. This letter should be mailed, not sent home with the student. Be sure to include the same details you would have addressed in a phone call.

- Show your concern for the student.

- State the specific problem the student is having.

- List the steps you have taken to help the student with the problem.

- Explain what you would like the parent to do.

- Let the parent know that you are confident that working together, the problem will be solved.

- Ask the parent to contact you by phone or note to discuss any comments she would like to make.

Contact either the father or the mother.

Teachers generally call the mother when there is a problem. Even if the father answers the phone, the teacher will often ask to speak to the mother. This reluctance to speak to the father has no place in a professional teacher's repertoire. Make as much effort to reach the father (at home or at work) as you do the mother.

When necessary, call the parent at work.

When you can't reach a parent at home by phone or through a note, your next step is to call the parent at work. Don't fall into the trap of feeling that you shouldn't "bother" a parent at work. Think back to the pediatrician analogy. Would a doctor hesitate to call a parent at work about a child's medical problem? Would you hesitate to call a parent at work if the child was physically ill? Your

Sample Letter to a Parent Who Is Hard to Reach

Dear Mr. and Mrs. McCafferty:

I'm writing because I'm concerned about how little work Danny has been doing at school. For the last two days, he has refused to do some of his assignments during class. As a result, I have had him stay in during recess to complete them. To help motivate him to do his work appropriately, I have told him he will receive a point each time he does his work in class. He knows that when he earns five points he will receive extra free time.

I would like your help in backing me up on this issue. Danny needs to know that his parents—as well as his teacher—insist that he does his work in school. Each day, I will send home a note to you, letting you know how well Danny is doing. Please sign the note and send it back with Danny the next day. I hope this will be enough to get Danny back on track.

Please call me if you have any questions. Danny is an intelligent, inquisitive boy. I'm sure that by working together we can help him do a better job in school. I will contact you next Monday to talk about how he is progressing.

Sincerely,

Mr. Elwood

behavioral and academic concerns about your student are every bit as important. Don't avoid action because you're afraid a parent might be angry. Make that phone call with the knowledge that it is your professional duty to do so. The assurance and competence you project when you speak with the parent will help defuse any resentment a parent may feel.

Call the student's emergency number.

The school has on record an emergency phone number for each child. Most often it is the number of a friend or relative who lives nearby. In those cases where a parent doesn't seem to react to your efforts at contacting her, calling this number is an effective method. When a neighbor rings the parent's doorbell to say the school is having a problem with her child, the parent will usually respond immediately.

Send a registered letter.

A registered letter can have an enormous impact on a parent who seems to be avoiding you. It emphasizes the importance of your message and also prevents a parent from saying he never received your communication.

Follow up on the initial contact.

If your child's teacher called you about a problem, wouldn't you want her to call again with a progress report? Wouldn't you want to know what was happening? Follow-up contact with parents is always necessary whether the problem has improved or not. Remember that you are building a relationship you want to grow and improve throughout the year. The parent needs to know that you will not go away—that you care too much about the student to give up.

Contact the parent when the problem behavior has improved.

It is very important for you to let the parent know that there is no longer a problem and then thank the parent for the support and help given. Let the parent know it was your teamwork that helped resolve the issue so quickly and satisfactorily. Most parents never receive supportive feedback from teachers. It's a real boost when they hear that their child has improved and that they played a part in that improvement.

Follow up with a phone call.
When making a call to parents about a student's improvement, be sure to include these points in your conversation:

- Describe the progress the student has made.

- Point out how the parent's cooperation helped the child.

■ Tell the parent that you will continue to stay in touch.

Teacher: Mr. Nelson, this is Ms. Jensen. I just wanted to let you know that since we last spoke, Brian has really improved. He is doing all his work. There is no arguing and no fighting. He seems much happier in class.

Parent: That's great news. He seems happier at home, too.

Teacher: I want to thank you for all the support you gave. By working with your son at home, and following through, you have helped him make some important changes. You should be pleased with the results.

Parent: Thank you. It was worth the effort, and Brian is proud of himself for improving.

Teacher: I'll continue to stay in touch. And if you ever have any questions or concerns, please feel free to call me. Again, thanks so much for your support.

Follow up with a letter.

Although a phone call is the best way to follow up with parents, you may in some circumstances prefer to send home a note. Include the same information that you would in a call.

Sample Follow-Up Letter

Dear Mr. Duffy,

Elliot has had perfect attendance all month. Thank you for cooperating with the school and for supervising him more closely. I know he will have an excellent year. Please call me if you have any concerns at all about his progress at school. I'll stay in touch with you, too.

Sincerely,

Miss Crowe

Contact the parent if the problem has not improved.

If the problem has not improved, you must contact the parent regarding further action. The goal of this phone call will be to agree upon the next steps both you and the parent will take. Once again, write down what you want to say before you make the call.

Begin with a statement of concern.

Teacher: Mrs. Carroll, this is Mr. Tanaka. I'm calling because I'm worried that Terry is still continuing to fight at school.

Describe the problem behavior.

Teacher: He lost his temper again at recess when he did not get his way in a game and he hit a child.

Describe what you have done.

Teacher: I've continued to speak with him and work with him on improving his behavior. We've also taken away recess when he does fight.

Get the parent's input.

Teacher: What do you do at home when you receive notes from me about his fighting?

Parent: I try to ground him. It really doesn't work because he gets so upset. I can't even keep him in his room. He gets so worked up, I can't deal with him.

Show your understanding and concern.

Teacher: I understand how difficult that must be.

Tell the parent what you will do and what kind of support you need.

Teacher: I feel that we need to work further to help Terry. I think the best thing we can do to help him now is for you to come in and talk with me and Mr. Lowes, our principal. Mr. Lowes is very skilled at helping teachers and parents deal with children who have trouble not fighting. I feel very confident that if you and I work together with him, we can all come up with a solution to help Terry stop his fighting.

Parent: Well, I hope you're right. But I don't know if anything will work. That's just the way Terry is.

Express your confidence.

Teacher: I understand how frustrated you are. That's why we have to work together to help him. As I said, Mr. Lowes and I have handled many students just like Terry, and I'm confident that we can help him have a better year. I'd like to meet as soon as possible. Could you come in tomorrow at 3:30?

File your notes and records.

Communication isn't complete until you've filed all notes and records pertaining to your parental contact. This includes your planning sheets, notes taken during the conversation, and any follow-up data you may have. See the guidelines on pages 134 to 137 for maintaining documentation records.

Contacting Parents at the First Sign of a Problem
REMINDERS

DO

➤ Use the "your own child" test when you are unsure about contacting a parent about a problem.

➤ Make a phone call your first-choice means of reaching a parent.

➤ Make every effort to contact a parent. Don't give up after one or two tries. You can reach a parent if you really want to.

➤ Always write down what you want to say before you phone a parent.

➤ Be prepared to describe the specific behavior that is causing problems.

➤ Let the parent know what steps you've already taken to correct the problem.

➤ Make sure you ask for the parent's suggestions for how to deal with the problem. Be prepared to adapt your efforts accordingly.

➤ Be prepared to tell the parent what you are planning to do about the problem.

➤ Let the parent know that you're confident the problem can be solved.

➤ Tell the parent there will be follow-up contact from you.

➤ Follow through with your promise!

(continued)

Contacting Parents at the
First Sign of a Problem
REMINDERS *(continued)*

DON'T

➤ Don't apologize for "bothering" the parent. Remember that you are acting in the child's best interests.

➤ Don't hesitate to call a parent at work if you can't reach her at home.

➤ Don't try to reach the student's mother only. Contact with fathers is also important.

➤ Don't make vague statements about the student's behavior.

Contacting Parents at the First Sign of a Problem CHECKLIST

Refer to this checklist each time you prepare to make initial contact with a parent about a problem.

Have you:

____ used the "your own child" test to help you decide whether or not to contact a parent?

____ written down all the points you want to cover with a parent?

____ aggressively tried to contact hard-to-reach parents?

____ included the student's father, as well as the mother, in problem-solving discussions?

____ made follow-up contact whether or not the problem has improved?

____ kept written records of all parent communication that has taken place?

____ kept copies of all notes you sent home and received from parents?

Conducting a Problem-Solving Conference 12

When a phone call or note to a parent doesn't solve a problem, or if a specific problem seems to warrant it, you need to schedule a face-to-face problem-solving conference. This chapter will help you plan and conduct the conference so that it will be more successful.

A problem-solving conference is your opportunity to meet with a parent and discuss a student's specific problem at school. The conference gives you a chance to gather information on the problem and present it to the parent in an organized, professional manner. It also provides an opportunity for you to listen to a parent's input and use that information to help the student. The goal of the conference is for parent and teacher to agree upon a plan of action for solving the student's specific problem.

Plan and conduct the conference.

Step 1: Decide who will be involved in the conference.

The first thing you need to consider is whether or not to include the student in a problem-solving conference. Some teachers try to include the student, others prefer not to. Use your own criteria to determine when the student's presence will be appropriate.

Here are some reasons teachers have for *not* including a student in a parent-teacher conference.

- Teachers may be concerned that the parent will not be able to openly discuss sensitive matters. Parents are often understandably concerned about hurting the child by discussing shortcomings or problems in front of him.

- There may be occasions when a teacher believes that the student's presence would be highly disruptive. This is particularly true in situations involving younger students who cannot sit still, or with older adolescents who may be hostile and verbally abusive throughout the meeting.

There are times, however, when it can be a very good idea to include a student in the conference, as follows. Keep in mind that a student's age and maturity must always be considered.

- Student input on the problem is needed. Sometimes you and the parent may need to hear the student's opinion about why he is having trouble in class or with homework. In addition, you may find that when teacher and parent are at a loss for solutions to a student's problem, the student himself may be able to provide an answer. The student may, for example, point out that a seating change could help, or that he needs to be given some specific study skills.

- Student commitment to change is needed. Having a student sit in on a parent-teacher conference can help make the student aware of the seriousness of the problem. When the student sees both the parent and teacher taking the time to discuss the problem, she may be convinced that change really is needed. Many teachers find that if they are using a home-school contract (see Chapter 13), it is important to have the student be a part of the process.

- You want to demonstrate that parent and teacher will work together to help the student. Many students, especially those involved in power struggles, try to play home and school against one another. If this is the case, it is vital that the student be present to hear both parent and teacher say that they will not tolerate the student's poor academic efforts or behavior problems. The student needs to see firsthand that the teacher and parent are a team and that there will be continued, consistent communication between home and school. The student needs to clearly understand that there will be corrective actions imposed at both home and school if he continues to behave inappropriately.

NOTE: If you do decide that a student's presence at a conference is warranted, you may want to meet with the parent first, then at a suitable point invite the student to come in and continue the conference.

Plan a team conference if it is warranted.

A team conference is one that involves more than one teacher. To help solve a student's problem, middle school and secondary school teachers, as well as some elementary teachers, often need to meet as a team with a parent. The goal of such a conference is not to gang up on a parent or overwhelm her with complaints, but to let the parent know that all of you are in this together, and that working as a team you can solve the student's problem.

In a team conference, one teacher must be designated to serve as facilitator. It will be the responsibility of this teacher to do the following:

Contact the parent to arrange a time for the conference.
Offer flexible time choices.

Conduct a preconference planning session.
Meeting with a group of teachers may be intimidating to a parent. It is vital that every teacher involved is in agreement ahead of time about the goals of the conference and the means of achieving these goals. The preconference planning session is the time to iron out these issues.

Follow these steps:

■ **Isolate one or two problems to be discussed.**
It is not productive to overwhelm a parent with everyone's complaints about the student. You don't want to turn the meeting into a dumping session. Even if there is more than one problem to deal with, narrow down the field to one or two to be discussed at this particular conference.

■ **Coordinate documentation that will be presented.**
The parent needs to see specific documentation of the student's problem behavior from each teacher involved.

■ **Write down all the points the team wishes to discuss.**
It is important that when the team of teachers meets with the parent, you've already worked out an agenda of points to cover. Use a Problem-Solving Conference Planning Sheet (see sample on page 163) to plan what will be said. It is the responsibility of the facilitator to keep the conference focused by sticking to the points on the agenda.

Lead the team conference.
Follow the guidelines for conducting a problem-solving conference. Plan to have all members of the team contribute by addressing different points.

The facilitator must see that the conference stays on track—that the teachers stick to addressing the issues that were planned. The facilitator should also pay attention to the parent's feelings.

In a team-conference situation, it is particularly important that teachers be sensitive to the parent. After all, there's only one of them and several of you. The facilitator must take special care to see that everyone listens to what the parent has to say. Above all, an atmosphere must be generated that instills confidence and optimism. Remember that your goal is to solve the problem and take steps toward getting parent support in the future.

> Whatever the variation of your problem-solving conference, the final two steps remain the same.

Step 2: Plan and write down what you will say to the parent.

Before your meeting, write down the important points you want to cover with the parent. Doing so will help you develop the skill and confidence that will allow you to conduct a more productive conference. Plan to take your notes with you for referral. Doctors look at notes during a consultation. Lawyers do, too. It's perfectly acceptable, and professional, to do so. It most likely will give parents even more confidence in you. The sample Problem-Solving Conference Planning Sheet on page 163 lists the points you should cover in the conference. Use a planning sheet like this to prepare for each problem-solving conference you hold.

As you prepare, keep in mind how a parent may feel at the conference. You are meeting because of a problem, so chances are the parent may be anxious, upset, or worried. Be sensitive to the parent's feelings. A friendly, positive atmosphere will produce more results than an intimidating setting. Once again, make a mental note to put yourself in the position of the parent. Ask yourself, *How would I feel if I were the parent in this situation? How would I want the teacher to treat me?* Then let that awareness guide your words and actions.

Step 3: Gather documentation.

An important part of a problem-solving conference is describing the specific problem and then presenting documentation. Parents often need to see proof

Sample Problem-Solving Conference Planning Sheet

Problem-Solving Conference Planning Sheet

Teacher _____ Grade _____

Student's Name _____

Parent(s) or Guardian _____

Date of conference _____

1. Begin with a statement of concern, updating the situation.

2. Describe the specific problem and present pertinent documentation.

3. Describe what you have already done to solve the problem.

4. Get parental input on the problem.

5. Get parental input on how to solve the problem.

6. Tell the parent what you will do to help solve the problem.

7. Explain what you need the parent to do to solve the problem.

8. Let the parent know you're confident that the problem can be worked out.

9. Tell the parent that there will be follow-up contact from you.

10. Recap the conference.

Notes: _____

_____

_____

that a problem does exist. Make sure you have all your documentation with you at the conference. Have it ordered chronologically so that you can present a clear picture to the parent of what has transpired.

Sample Problem-Solving Conference

Here are step-by-step guidelines for conducting a problem-solving conference:

1. **Begin with a statement of concern, updating the situation.**
   Because a problem-solving conference can be stressful and upsetting to parents, it is important that you begin the conversation by showing your concern for the student rather than just by bluntly stating the problem.

   "Mr. Stein, I'm still worried about John's misbehavior at recess."

   "Mrs. Davis, I'm still concerned about Jenny's inability to turn in her homework assignments."

2. **Describe the specific problem and present pertinent documentation.**
   Explain in specific, observable terms what the child did or did not do. Remember that an observable behavior is one that you can watch going on, such as failing to turn in assignments or fighting. Show the parent your records that document the child's behavior. Make sure the documentation is not judgmental and is impartial.

   "This week John was involved in four fights. You can see here that he was sent to the office twice on Tuesday and again on Wednesday and Thursday."

   "You can see from these records that Jenny did not turn in any math assignments this week."

3. **Describe what you have already done to solve the problem.**
   As you show your documentation, explain how you have dealt with the problem. If appropriate, refer to your classroom discipline plan and point out that you have been acting in accordance with that plan.

   "As you know, I have given John detention each time he's been involved in a fight."

   "I have reminded Jenny that her final report card grade will drop if homework is not turned in. I have also sent her to detention to finish her work."

4. **Get parental input on the problem.**
   Listen carefully to what the parent has to say. As you listen, take special care to show the parent that you respect his opinion. Too often, parents and teachers don't show respect to one another. As a professional, it's up to you to take the lead by showing parents you value what they say. If appropriate, be prepared to adapt your disciplinary strategies to incorporate the parent's comments and suggestions.

Here are some questions you may want to ask.

"Has your child had similar problems in the past?" (It may be useful to examine school records to determine if the child did have problems previously and if the parent was aware of them.)

"Does your child have similar problems at home?"

"Why do you feel that your child is having this problem?"

"Have there been any changes (divorce, separation, siblings, a move) at home that could be affecting your child's behavior?"

5. Get parental input on how to solve the problem.
Most parents know their child better than anyone and might have good ideas about how to solve specific problems. Chances are, you'll hear something like "Well, I guess I'll have to do something to make sure he behaves in school." That's your opportunity to move in and enlist their help. Seize the moment.
   Ask the parent:

"Are you dealing with this problem at home as well? How have you handled it so far?"

"How do you feel we can work together to help your child solve this problem?"

If a suggestion seems to make sense, show your willingness to use it in your own disciplinary strategies.

"This seems like a good way of dealing with this. Maybe I can do something similar at school. Let me think about this, and I'll get back to you."

6. Tell the parent what you will do to help solve the problem.
You've already explained what you have previously done and what effect it has had. Now explain your new plan of action to resolve this issue. Let the parent know exactly what you are going to do. Then check for understanding to make sure everything is clearly understood.

"Mr. Stein, since this problem has continued, I am going to change the disciplinary corrective actions for John. From now on, each time he fights he will be sent immediately to the principal and you will be called. He won't receive any reminders first, and he won't be sent to detention."

"Mrs. Davis, since the problem wasn't solved, I am going to develop a behavior contract for Jenny. Every time she fails to turn in homework, she will go to detention.

Every time she does turn in her homework, she will receive a point. Ten points and she's earned a bonus grade."

NOTE: If there is to be a home-school contract, introduce it now. (See Chapter 13 for complete guidelines.)

7. **Explain what you need the parent to do to solve the problem.**
Now you must explain, just as carefully, what you would like the parent to do to help solve the problem. Be careful not to dispense general parenting advice. Be very specific in your requests for support. Make sure the parent knows that you are asking for help with a specific problem rather than for a change of his parenting style.

"Mr. Stein, we need to work together to help John improve his behavior. His fights are completely unacceptable. Any time you are called about a fight, I'd appreciate it if you would follow through at home with your own disciplinary measures. Taking away privileges often works to convince children that you mean business. Whatever you choose to do, remember that you must do it consistently and not back down."

"Mrs. Davis, it is extremely important that we work together to help Jenny get into the habit of turning in all her homework assignments. To do this, I would like you to check each night to see that all assignments are completed. Your signature on her homework will show me that you've looked it over. Please understand, I don't expect you to correct the work, just to make sure that it's complete."

Pay close attention to any parental roadblocks that might appear. (Does the parent sound overwhelmed? Negative? Confused?) Use your communication skills to move the parent past the roadblock.

8. **Let the parent know you're confident that the problem can be worked out.**
Well-chosen words will punctuate your message with assurance.

- Use the word *confident* when you speak to the parent.

- Use both the parent's name and the student's name.

- Reassure the parent that you are experienced in dealing with this type of problem.

"Mr. Stein, I am confident that together we can make this a better year for John. I've dealt with many children who have had this problem, and I can assure you that we will be able to turn things around if we are united in our efforts."

"Mrs. Davis, I feel confident that with both of our efforts we can help Jenny develop more responsible homework habits."

9. Tell the parent that there will be follow-up contact from you.

A parent needs to know that you are going to stay involved. Provide this reassurance by giving a specific date for a follow-up call or note.

"Mr. Stein, I am going to call you next Monday evening to let you know how things are working out for John."

"Mrs. Davis, I'll give you a call Friday night to let you know how the week went."

10. Recap the conference.

Write down all agreed-upon actions. Whenever communication takes place, there is always the question of whether each party understands what the other is saying. To avoid confusion and assure that the message was clear, you may need to clarify all agreements. You can do this by restating and writing down what you are going to do and what the parent is going to do. Keep this information in your files. If you feel that it will be helpful to the parent, say that you will mail home a copy of this agreement in a day or two.

Teacher: We've agreed to a number of things today. I'll put our decisions in writing and send them home to you. Here's what I've agreed to do: I am going to change the disciplinary corrective actions for John. From now on, each time he fights he will be sent immediately to the principal and you will be called. No more reminders. No more detention.

The teacher writes while speaking.

Parent: And I've agreed to take privileges away from him at home anytime I'm called about John fighting.

The teacher continues writing.

Teacher: Okay, I've got it all written down. Mr. Stein, I'd like to thank you for helping me put this plan of action together. Now John will know that we're working together to solve this problem.

Another example:

Teacher: Okay, Mrs. Davis. We've agreed to a plan of action here today that will help Jenny do a better job on homework. Here's what I will be doing: I'm going to develop a behavior contract for Jenny. Every time she doesn't turn in her homework she will have detention. Every time she does turn in her homework she will receive a point. Ten points and she will earn a bonus grade.

To be certain that we both understand what will be happening, I'm going to write down what both of us have agreed to.

The teacher begins writing.

Now, what will you be doing each night to help Jenny handle homework better?

Parent: Every night, I'm going to check all of Jenny's completed homework. And I'll sign each paper to show you that I've seen it.

The teacher continues writing.

Teacher: That's going to be really helpful. When you check her homework each night, Jenny will better understand that both of us are committed to her success in school. I'm sure we'll soon see a difference in her homework habits.

11. Close the conference.

Thank the parent for coming in to meet with you. Let the parent know that taking the time to improve the child's educational experience is time well spent.

Conducting a Problem-Solving Conference
REMINDERS

DO

➤ Bring documentation with you to the conference.

➤ Be sensitive to a parent's feelings throughout the conference. Listen carefully and make comments to demonstrate that sensitivity.

➤ Consider whether or not you want the student to be present at the conference.

➤ Explain problems to parents in observable terms. Be specific.

➤ Listen to a parent's comments and suggestions. Show your willingness to incorporate them into your plan of action.

➤ Give parents the materials they need to support your plan of action: stickers, checklists, award certificates.

➤ Leave parents with hope and confidence.

DON'T

➤ Don't arrive at the conference unprepared. Make sure you have written down all the points you want to cover.

➤ Don't have a parent sit on a student-sized chair while you sit in the teacher's chair.

➤ Don't dredge up incidents from the past.

➤ Don't overwhelm parents by presenting too many problems. Two or three examples are enough.

➤ Don't make idle disciplinary threats.

➤ Don't be condescending. A parent may have a valuable perspective on the problem.

➤ Don't talk about other students if the parent tries to divert the conversation by placing blame on others.

Conducting a Problem-Solving Conference
CHECKLIST

Refer to this checklist each time you prepare for a problem-solving conference.

Have you:

____ written down what you will say to the parent at the conference?

____ decided what you will do to help solve the problem?

____ decided what you want the parent to do?

____ reminded yourself to listen to what the parent says—to treat him with respect?

____ organized the documentation you need to bring to the conference?

____ reviewed effective listening skills?

____ decided whether or not to include the student in the conference?

If the conference involves more than one teacher, **have you:**

____ designated one teacher to be the facilitator?

____ arranged to hold a preconference planning meeting with all teachers involved?

____ gathered documentation from all teachers involved?

____ decided, with the other teachers, on one or two problems to focus on?

____ written down what will be said to the parent at the conference?

Using a Home-School Contract

CHAPTER
13

It's one thing for a parent to agree at a conference to work with you to solve a student's specific problem. It's sometimes quite another to actually succeed at making this partnership work. After the conference is over, after the parent goes home, how do you ensure success? How do you make certain that you meet the goals you and the parent set during the conference? How can you make certain you get the support you need?

The best way to successfully structure a parent's efforts with yours is by using a home-school contract. This chapter will explain the nature of this contract and detail the steps for its construction and use as follows:

- What is a home-school contract?

- When should you use a home-school contract?

- Why is a home-school contract effective?

- How to write and present a home-school contract.

- Daily communication is a must.

What is a home-school contract?

A home-school contract is a written agreement between teacher, student, and parent. The contract states that the student agrees to a specific behavior. If the student complies with the terms of the contract, she will earn praise and rewards from both the teacher and parent.

Be sure the student understands that both parent and teacher are working together in a team effort to solve a problem. The student knows that if she chooses not to comply with the contract, she can expect predetermined corrective actions from both school and home. The success of a home-school contract demands that both parent and teacher cooperate and consistently enforce it. A home-school contract is an effective technique to use with both elementary and secondary school students.

The examples of home-school contracts presented in this book are based on the behavior management techniques developed in *Assertive Discipline*. While the balanced system of supportive feedback for appropriate behavior and consistent corrective actions for inappropriate behavior established therein is extremely effective, your specific home-school contracts should reflect your approach to behavior management. You are encouraged, however, to establish a discipline plan that doesn't only discipline misbehavior but also rewards improved and appropriate behavior. Furthermore, it is important that the home-school contract you establish suits your personal teaching style and the parent's personal parenting style.

When should you use a home-school contract?

Use a home-school contract to correct behavioral, academic, or homework problems for any age level. A contract is warranted when you can answer yes to any of these questions:

- Have you tried to solve the problem through other means, without success?

- Could the student benefit from a structured system of supportive feedback and corrective actions?

- Does the parent need daily feedback regarding the student's behavior at school?

- Do you suspect that the student receives little supportive feedback at home?

- Have the student's parents asked for help from you in solving the student's problem?

Why is a home-school contract effective?

A home-school contract helps the teacher, parent, and student focus on a specific problem that needs to be solved. Vague comments like "He's always getting into trouble" or "Her behavior is just impossible" don't help a problem get solved.

Sample Home-School Contract

Home-School Contract

Jeffrey Smith promises to stay out of fights on the school yard. Each day the student does as agreed, he can expect the following actions to take place.

From the teacher:

1. Verbal reinforcement.

2. One point for each day of appropriate behavior. When 10 points are earned, Jeffrey may spend an extra hour on the computer.

3. A note home to parents telling them of Jeffrey's successful day.

From the parent:

1. Verbal reinforcement.

2. One point for each day of appropriate behavior. When 10 points are earned, Jeffrey may invite a friend to dinner and a movie.

Each day the student does not do as agreed, he can expect the following actions to take place.

From the teacher:

1. Fifteen minutes detention after school.

2. A note home to parents telling them about Jeffrey's behavior that day.

From the parent:

1. Loss of TV and phone privileges that night.

The contract will be in effect from October 6 to October 17.

Parent's signature: _____

Teacher's signature: _____

Student's signature: _____

You need to pinpoint exactly what behavior you want from a student. The home-school contract will help you and the parent do just that.

A home-school contract is really a plan of action for helping a student improve his behavior. Parent and teacher decide together which steps they will take to solve the problem. You as the teacher may stress the importance of consistency when disciplining a child for inappropriate behavior. You may stress the value and benefit of supportive feedback and encourage the parent to frequently reward the child for appropriate behavior. You may not, however, decide what the parent should do. The home-school contract has to be a true collaborative effort between teacher and parent, where both parties play a part in the outcome.

A home-school contract requires the parent to state, in writing, that she agrees to fulfill the obligations of the contract. Teachers' attempts to solve a student's problem often fail because parents don't carry through at home. The contract will help structure disciplinary responses for parents who don't know what to do to help their child. It gives parents a framework to follow and teachers a means of keeping track of what's going on at home. Once the parent signs the agreement, the teacher is within his rights to inquire if the parent is following through as planned.

Keep in mind that the effectiveness of the contract depends greatly on how it is composed. A home-school contract is not a prefabricated document to be used in any situation with any student and parent. It is a very personal agreement, custom-tailored to meet the needs of a particular situation. Its content is defined cooperatively by the teacher and the parent. A home-school contract is not a means to tell a parent how to raise her child and to impose your own discipline plan. It is not a forum for dispensing parenting advice and changing a parent's child-rearing practices. Instead it is an attempt to incorporate the parent's usual child-rearing practices at home into your disciplinary efforts at school to solve a very specific problem.

How to write and present a home-school contract.

A home-school contract is a collaborative effort between teacher and parent and should be dealt with as part of a problem-solving conference. Here are the steps to explaining and writing a home-school contract.

Step 1: Introduce the concept of a home-school contract to the parent.

A careful explanation of the contract is vital. Chances are the parent has never even seen one before. Explain right away that the contract is an agreement between you, the parent, and the student and that the purpose of the contract is to help the student succeed in school. Be sensitive. Once again, put yourself in the parent's position and realize that this procedure at first might seem a bit intimidating. Let the parent know that you have successfully used home-school contracts before.

> "I feel that the best way to help *(student's name)* is for us to put together a home-school contract for him. A home-school contract is a written agreement between me, you, and your child. The contract will state that *(student's name)* agrees to a specific behavior. If he complies with the terms of the contract, he will earn praise and rewards from both you and me. If he chooses not to comply with the contract, he will receive predetermined corrective actions from both school and home.

> "The reason a home-school contract can be so successful is that your child will know that we're working together to help him solve his problem. Whenever he misbehaves during the day, I'll let you know about it. Likewise, when he behaves appropriately, you'll know about that, too.

> "I've used home-school contracts many times in the past and have found them to be successful.

> "This is the contract form."

Show the contract to the parent and let her look it over.

Step 2: Determine how you want the student to behave.

Work with the parent to focus on one or two specific areas of concern. (These should be the same problems you presented to the parent at the beginning of the problem-solving conference.) For example: "I'm concerned about Jeffrey's fighting at recess"; or "I'm very concerned that Serena is still not completing her homework assignments."

"Let's begin the contract by focusing on exactly what we need your child to do at school. We've been talking about his problems with *(state problem)*. We will write down on the contract that *(student's name)* will promise to *(state desired behavior)*. Do you have any questions about this?"

Step 3: Explain the corrective actions you will provide if the student does not comply with the contract.

You must decide what you will do at school if the student chooses not to do what is expected. You should determine your disciplinary measures before the parent arrives for the conference. Explain to the parent that you will use corrective actions each time the student does not comply with the contract.

"I want your child to clearly understand that we cannot allow him to continue a behavior that's not in his best interests. Therefore, I want to spell out exactly what I will do if he chooses not to follow the promise he made in the contract. Here's what will happen at school: Each time he does not comply with the contract, he will stay after school for detention. In addition, of course, a note will go home letting you know what happened."

Write the corrective actions in the contract.

If the parent strongly objects to the disciplinary measures you choose, you need to pause to discuss this. If the parent's objections seem valid, be prepared to adjust your course of action.

For example, if the parent objects because staying after school for detention interferes with a student's need for medical attention, try to agree on a different corrective action. If, however, the parent objects because staying after school for detention will interfere with a social activity, explain that missing the activity will make the corrective action work.

In any case, don't just impose any part of the contract on the parent. The resentment that may ensue will endanger the effectiveness of the entire contract. Always invite, respect, and accept a parent's input.

Step 4: Help the parent choose the corrective actions to provide if the student does not comply with the contract.

The success of the home-school contract depends upon the parent's willingness to follow through at home. This means a parent must be willing to discipline the child if he does not follow the terms of the contract. Be aware that this is often difficult for parents to do effectively. Their disciplinary measures may be extremely inconsistent.

Parents must let their child know that they will not tolerate misbehavior at school. This part of the contract is vital. You must impress upon parents the importance of consistent follow-through.

> "Next we need to spell out exactly what you will do at home if this misbehavior continues. You need to choose a corrective action that *(student's name)* will receive each time he misbehaves. Choose something that you know he won't like. Parents often choose corrective actions such as loss of TV or phone privileges, grounding, or restricted use of a bicycle or other sports equipment. Think for a minute about what you might choose."

Write down the corrective actions the parent will use. Discuss the options if the parent is unsure. Try to guide the parent to choose corrective actions that are not too harsh. It is not the severity of the disciplinary measure that ensures its success but the consistency with which it is imposed. Strongly discourage the parent from using punishment that is physically or emotionally harmful. Make sure the parent understands that corrective actions are not meant to be punishment at all, but a reminder for the child to change his behavior.

Step 5: Explain the supportive feedback you *will give* to the student for appropriate behavior.

Motivating students to change their behavior requires supportive feedback. A home-school contract must specify the rewards that you, the teacher, will offer at school when the student behaves appropriately.

The best form of positive support, particularly for younger students, is verbal reinforcement. The contract must include that you will consistently reinforce the student when he complies with the terms of the contract. In addition, you may want to couple your verbal reinforcement with tangible rewards. Think about what the student would like to earn. What would motivate him to give that extra bit of effort? You may even want to ask the student what he would like to earn. The more involved the student is in this process, the more success you will have.

Decide on the tangible rewards you intend to use before meeting with the parent.

Sample Ideas for Tangible Rewards

Ideas for Tangible Rewards

In addition to verbal reinforcement, you may want to motivate students with small tangible rewards. Here are some ideas.

For elementary students:

➤ Healthy snacks

➤ Class monitor

➤ First in line

➤ Lunch with teacher

➤ Free reading time

➤ Extra computer time

➤ Choose PE activity

➤ Award certificate

➤ Stickers

For middle and secondary students:

➤ Extra computer time

➤ Gift certificate from a fast-food restaurant

➤ Free admission to a school function

➤ Right to be first to leave class

➤ Gift certificate to school store or another store

"I feel very strongly that it is important for your child to receive supportive feedback when he behaves appropriately. Here's what I plan to do: Whenever he does what we have asked him to do, I will let him know that I recognize and appreciate what he has done. I want him to feel proud of his achievement and to understand that appropriate behavior will earn attention. In addition, I will give him an extra incentive. I know that your son would like to earn extra time on the computer. Each day he complies with the contract, I will give him a point. When he gets five points, he will earn 15 minutes of computer time. I think he will want to work toward this reward. Do you agree?

"Now let's fill in these provisions on the contract."

Should the parent offer strong objections to the particular supportive feedback you choose, discuss it. If a parent's objections seem valid, be prepared to adjust your plans accordingly. For example, a student may spend many hours at the computer at home, and thus the parent may not want him to earn any more time at the computer at all. Since it is not your place to suggest that the parent restrict computer time at home unless it interferes with your student's performance at school, it might be more effective to try and agree upon another reward. If, however, the parent objects to the fact that the student receives any reward at all for appropriate behavior, calmly explain that supportive feedback will help the student continue his efforts to improve his behavior.

Step 6: Help the parent choose the supportive feedback to provide when the child complies with the contract.

Parents need to understand that their words of praise and support are very important to their child. Emphasize clearly that the parent really is the most important person in the child's life and that her praise means a lot.

"I've told you about the supportive feedback I will give *(student's name)* each day that his behavior improves at school. It's just as important that you give supportive feedback at home, too. He really does care about what you think of him. You can do so much to encourage his efforts. I would like to write down on the contract that each day your son behaves, you promise to give him lots of well-deserved praise.

"In addition, you may find that it would help to give an extra-special reward for good behavior. Choose something that you know your child would like and that you are comfortable giving. You may want to do the same thing I'm doing at school. Each day he behaves appropriately, he will earn a point from you. When he earns five points, he receives the reward. Keep in mind that the gift of your own time might be the most valuable reward you can give. Lots of students really enjoy earning special time alone with Mom or Dad.

"Here are some ideas that kids often appreciate. *(Give parent some age-appropriate suggestions. Be sensitive to the parent's financial circumstances.)*

➤ Going out for lunch with Mom or Dad.

➤ Having a friend over for dinner.

➤ Staying up late one night.

➤ Going out to dinner.

➤ Buying a new book.

➤ Spending an hour of uninterrupted time with Mom or Dad."

Step 7: Decide on the duration of the contract.

You need to decide how long a contract will be in effect: one week, two weeks, or three weeks. Consider the age of your student and the behavior you are dealing with. Fill in this information on the contract.

Step 8: Sign and present the contract.

The home-school contract must be signed by all involved parties: student, teacher, and parent. At this point, the student may be included in the conference. Carefully explain the terms of the contract to him. Make sure that you and the parent present the contract together, clarifying the fact that you're working as a team.

Show a warm, positive attitude here. Let the student know that you regard the contract as an opportunity to change things for the better, not as a punishment.

"As you know, your mother *(or father)* and I are very concerned about *(state the problem)*. You have received detention many times, but the problem hasn't been solved.

"We have put together a contract that will help you behave appropriately at school. This contract is an agreement between you, your mother, and me about what will happen when you do and do not behave.

"Let's read it together."

Read the terms of the contract, making sure the student understands every point.

"As you can see, when you sign this contract, you agree to *(state desired behavior)*. Each day that you behave according to the contract, you will receive *(state your supportive feedback)* from me at school and *(state parent's supportive feedback)* from your mother at home. On the other hand, on days that you do not comply with the contract, you can expect to receive *(state your corrective actions)* from me at school and *(state parent's corrective actions)* from your mother at home. Your mother has agreed to follow through with these corrective actions because she cares about you and wants you to succeed at school.

"This is how the contract will work: Each day, I will be sending home a note to your mother telling her how the day went. If everything went well—that is, if you behaved according to the contract—I will tell her so. If the day did not go well, I'll tell her that, too. Do you have any questions you'd like to ask me or your mother?"

Before closing the conference, make sure once again that everyone clearly understands the terms of the contract. Reassure the parent that the next day she will receive a note from you updating the student's progress. End the meeting on a positive, enthusiastic note. Everyone should know that you expect success.

Daily communication is a must.

Once you've filled out and signed the contract, you need to decide how you will communicate with parents. In order to enforce the terms of the contract, you will need to be in daily contact with parents. The best method of daily communication is a home-school note. Each day the contract is in effect, send home a note letting the parent know how the student behaved in school that day. Include in your note:

- Date

- How the student behaved that day

- Actions you took (supportive feedback or corrective actions)

- What the parent needs to do at home (supportive feedback or corrective actions)

Sample Home-School Contract Daily Contact Sheet

Home-School Contract
Daily Contact Sheet

Student's name _____

Date _____

Dear _____

— Today your child behaved according to the terms of the contract. I have given the supportive feedback that we agreed upon. Please follow through at home with your supportive feedback.

— Today your child did not behave according to the terms of the contract. I have taken the corrective actions that we agreed upon. Please follow through at home with your corrective actions.

Please get in touch with me if you have any questions or would like to talk about the contract.

Sincerely,

Additional comments: _____

_____

_____

_____

_____

Using a Home-School Contract
REMINDERS

DO

➤ Use a home-school contract when you want to ensure a parent's continuing involvement in solving a student's problem.

➤ Write the contract with the parent. Take all comments and suggestions seriously. If appropriate, change your course of action accordingly.

➤ Decide ahead of time which supportive feedback and corrective actions you will use.

➤ Prepare to give the parent guidelines and suggestions for choosing the supportive feedback and corrective actions she will use.

➤ Think carefully about how you will present the concept of a contract to a parent. Make notes on what you will say.

➤ Be sure to emphasize to the parent how important his praise and support is to the child. Consistent follow-through is the key to making the contract work.

➤ Send home a note each day telling the parent how the student behaved.

➤ Always follow through with your plan. When the student misbehaves, use the corrective action you agreed upon. When the student behaves appropriately, she deserves lots of praise.

(continued)

Using a Home-School Contract
REMINDERS *(continued)*

DON'T

➤ Don't feel that using a home-school contract is asking too much of a parent. This kind of structured involvement is exactly what many parents need to help them discipline their child at home for misbehavior at school. It will also help ensure that the student receives lots of positive attention at home for improvement at school.

➤ Don't hesitate to call a parent any time you have a question regarding follow-through at home. If you have a feeling that the parent isn't living up to the terms of the contract, give him a call. Remember that the parent's signature constitutes a promise of action. Likewise, don't hesitate to call with good news either. A parent will be most happy to hear from you when things are improving.

Using a Home-School Contract
CHECKLIST

Refer to this checklist when you prepare to use a home-school contract.

Have you:

___ decided on the specific behavior you want from the student?

___ decided before the conference on the corrective actions you will include in the contract?

___ decided before the conference on the supportive feedback you will include in the contract?

___ reviewed the guidelines for writing a home-school contract?

___ made some notes about what you will say to the parent(s)?

Providing Support for Parents' Disciplinary Efforts

No matter what efforts you make at school, without parent support it will be very difficult for you to get some of your students to behave appropriately and improve academically. Unfortunately, the parents of many of these students are often unable to influence and discipline their own children. In other words, students who need assistance the most at home may get it the least—not because their parents don't want to help, but most likely because they don't know how. To increase these parents' ability to support you at school, you may need to give them some simple strategies to use at home.

Please note the following qualifications:

- Parents must want your help. Do not give parents advice on behavior management unless they have indicated to you that they want to hear your suggestions.

- Do not work with parents on your own if you suspect the child or parent has emotional problems. Keep in mind that you are not a therapist or counselor and that it is not appropriate for you to intervene on your own in circumstances that require professional help. If you suspect that a student, or a parent, needs counseling, involve the school psychologist, counselor, and/or principal.

Begin by once again impressing upon parents that the home environment is one of the most important influences on a child's academic performance and social behavior. A parent's influence can significantly increase a child's interest and success in school. This is true at any age and grade level. Parents need to take the time and make the effort at home to support their children's work at school. It is never too early or too late to get involved.

Make sure the parent understands that you do not want to dispense general parenting advice. Instead, what you want to do is increase the parent's ability to influence the child's performance at school. You are enlisting the parent's help for a specific problem because he is in the unique position to provide this help.

Your attitude has to reflect that you consider the parent the expert on his child. His expertise has been honed by years of experience. His expertise has raised a child with unique qualities beyond the specific behavioral problem you are dealing with.

You, on the other hand, have been trained to use certain behavior management approaches in the classroom. With your guidance, a parent can adapt these techniques for use at home.

Two experts working together can and will support the child to succeed in school.

In this chapter, you will find the following suggestions to help parents back you up at home by supporting your classroom disciplinary measures:

- Provide parents with skills to support your classroom discipline efforts.

- Help parents improve personal relationships with their children.

- Determine if academic assistance is needed.

- Make follow-up contact with parents.

The approaches suggested are simple and straightforward yet extremely effective. However, the following list is by no means exclusive. There are many more techniques available that may be equally effective. Be sure to use your professional judgment when deciding which technique you will present to a parent. In most cases, there's no need for the parent to change his approach to parenting. Present these strategies as helpful hints to be incorporated into the parent's personal parenting style to make it more effective and increase positive influence over his child.

Provide parents with skills to support your classroom discipline efforts.

When you speak with parents, explain that you will be working as a team to help their child improve her behavior. Make parents aware that this kind of teamwork sends a strong message to a child that her parents and the teacher are truly concerned about her success in school, at home, and in life.

Here are some techniques you can offer parents.

1. **Clearly tell your child exactly how you expect her to behave at school.**
   The first skill parents must learn is to clearly communicate how they expect their child to behave at school. Most parents who have trouble disciplining their children are not firm, clear, and direct about what they expect their child to do. Instead, these parents beg, plead, or use empty threats. Frustrated parents often lose their temper and end up yelling at their children. Emotional responses do not get results. They do not help teach a child to behave appropriately, and they leave the child without clear direction.

   Parents need to address the problematic behavior specifically, and impress upon their children in a firm yet calm manner that they won't allow their children to continue acting this way at school.

2. **Avoid arguments. Use the broken-record technique.**
   Parents often fall into the trap of arguing with their child whenever they ask the child to do anything. Arguing is not useful. Nobody wins. Parents must stick to their point. A technique called the "broken record" will help these parents avoid fruitless arguments while remaining calm.

   The parent keeps repeating what she wants. Every time the child argues, the parent responds with a calm but firm "I understand, but I expect you to . . ." If the child continues to argue after using the broken-record technique three times, the parent needs to postpone the conversation until later.

   The broken-record technique can help a parent avoid being dragged into a pointless debate and can help focus the child on the desired behavior.

3. **Back up words with disciplinary action.**
   Parents need to understand that simply demanding that their child behave at school may not be enough to ensure that it happens. Parents must learn to back up their words with actions to let the child know they are serious. This means a parent must be willing to impose corrective actions when the child chooses to misbehave. If the parent doesn't follow through, the child may not either.

   As stated in Chapter 13, the corrective action a parent uses must be something the child does not like, but it must never be physically or psychologically harmful. Suggest taking away privileges, such as watching TV, using the computer, or talking on the phone. Grounding is often effective. With younger children, grounding can mean being restricted to their room without TV for a short amount of time. For older children, grounding can mean not visiting with friends for a certain number of days.

The disciplinary measure must be used consistently. Each time the child chooses to misbehave, he must be given the corrective action. Make sure the parent understands that it is not the severity of a corrective action but its consistency that makes it effective.

It is vital that the parent remains calm when disciplining the child. The corrective action is not meant as punishment but rather to help the child choose more appropriate behavior in the future. Therefore, it is also important that the parent does not carry grudges. The matter must be over and done with once the disciplinary measure has been carried out.

4. **Know what to do when your child begins testing you.**

When parents begin setting limits and backing up their words with actions, the child will often try to manipulate the parent into backing down by crying, getting angry, or becoming defiant. It's a good idea to prepare parents for this possibility.

No matter how the child reacts to the chosen disciplinary measure, the parent must remain firm and follow through consistently.

5. **Acknowledge your child for appropriate behavior.**

As a teacher, you know that corrective actions can stop an unwanted behavior, but that supportive feedback is the key to changing behavior. Parents need to understand that it's just as important for them to give supportive feedback at home as it is for you to give it at school. Unfortunately, parents who are frustrated with their children's behavior may behave negatively when they relate to their children. It is vital that parents understand that they must balance their disciplinary corrective actions with supportive feedback if they are going to teach their child how to behave in a more positive manner at school. This is a very critical point that must be explained carefully.

Suggest to parents that they praise their child for appropriate behavior. Impress upon them one more time how important parents are to their children and how much their praise will mean.

Tell parents how helpful it is to combine praise with special privileges or rewards, like staying up late one night, getting extra computer time, or going out to lunch.

Whatever privilege or reward the parent picks, it must be given consistently. The child must know that just as he can expect a disciplinary action for inappropriate behavior, he can also expect lots of praise and support for good behavior.

Help parents improve personal relationships with their children.

Parental support of a child's work at school is important. Reaching out to a child to listen and learn about his life at school can improve a child's interest in and performance at school.

Many students feel that their parents show no interest in their performance at school and, in fact, don't really care about them at all. Obviously, this is not true. The vast majority of parents care deeply about their children and want to do whatever is in their power to help their children succeed in school.

Suggest to parents that they take five minutes a day to do any of the following:

- Ask about the day at school.

- Talk about special school events.

- Just talk about anything.

Advise parents to listen intently when the child talks and nod or ask questions to show interest. The child may begin simply by telling facts about a subject, but as parents demonstrate their attentiveness, the door is opened to increased understanding and sharing of the child's inner life.

Conversations like these can do wonders. They can make a child feel important and valued, they can improve the relationship between parent and child, and they can show that the parent cares.

Suggest to parents that they turn off the TV during dinner and just talk with their children so that they can listen and learn.

Determine if academic assistance is needed.

At the root of some discipline problems lies an academic weakness. For example, if a student comes to school unprepared, without completed homework, the student may easily stray off the task during class. If appropriate, you may want to suggest that the parent provide homework support in tandem with the disciplinary techniques you've recommended. This may take the form of structuring time for the student to do homework (see Chapter 7) or considering after-school tutoring programs, either at school or privately.

Make follow-up contact with parents.

Be sure to give parents a follow-up call in a few days to let them know whether or not the student's behavior at school is improving. If problems are continuing, you may want to use a home-school contract (see Chapter 13).

Providing Support for Parents' Disciplinary Efforts
REMINDERS

DO

➤ Let parents know that if they agree to it, you will provide suggestions for solving their child's behavioral problems.

➤ Clearly explain to parents how important it is that they follow through with both corrective actions and supportive feedback.

➤ Suggest that parents reach out to their children and take a more active interest in their children's lives.

➤ Put yourself in the parent's position throughout conversations with them. Recognize that it may not be easy to receive advice on handling one's own children. Above all, be sensitive to this issue.

DON'T

➤ Don't give parents advice unless you know they want your suggestions.

➤ Don't work with parents on your own if you suspect that the child has emotional problems. Involve the psychologist, counselor, or administrator in any efforts you make.

Providing Support for
Parents' Disciplinary Efforts
CHECKLIST

Refer to this checklist each time you plan to advise a parent on behavior management techniques to use at home.

Have you:

___ made sure that the parent wants your advice on disciplining her child?

___ determined to the best of your ability that the child or parent does not have emotional problems that should be dealt with by a counselor?

___ reviewed the guidelines for using the techniques presented in this chapter?

Dealing With Difficult Situations

If you haven't already, sooner or later you will encounter parents who make things difficult for you. They may be angry at you or angry at the school. They may be upset by years of perceived (or real) injustices. They may be frustrated by their inability to deal with their children, or they may just be overwhelmed by the stress in their own lives. Whatever the reason, these are parents whose roadblocks threaten to undermine your teaching efforts.

At first, these roadblocks may seem insurmountable. They may appear to be so established that you're sure you've come to a dead end with this parent. Not true. You may be detoured, but you can get back on track.

This book has stressed the importance of developing an effective attitude, holding fast to professionalism and confidence, and recognizing roadblocks. Make sure you are honest about your attitudes toward a parent. Once you recognize a problem that may stand in your way, it will be much easier to deal with the parent in a sensitive yet effective manner.

This chapter presents several ways in which your preparation and the right attitude will see you through even the most difficult situations. They are:

- Prepare in advance to handle angry or distraught parents.

- Use specific communication techniques for difficult situations.

- Use specialized techniques with the most difficult parents.

- Difficult situations *can* be handled successfully.

Now is when you will really see the benefits of what you've learned in *Parents on Your Side*. When you know that you can deal effectively with the most difficult situations, you will know you have learned your techniques well.

Prepare in advance to handle angry or distraught parents.

> "This parent came in and just read me the riot act. I had lowered her daughter's grade on a term paper because it was turned in late. But according to the parent, I was to blame. She said I was such a lousy teacher that her daughter didn't know how to do the work. I didn't know how to respond. I was just shaking. And the worst part of it was that all of my students were watching!"

You can't avoid situations like these. You can't even anticipate them. When they occur, you have to be prepared to stand your ground and proceed with confidence. You have to show respect and practice sensitivity at all times, even if a parent does not. You have a lot riding on this moment, and you need to handle it carefully, professionally, and effectively. Your behavior toward the parent has to be exemplary. The well-being of your students depends upon your ability to reach the parent right then and there.

As you've probably told your students, the more thoroughly you learn your lessons, the easier they will be to apply. Those same words pertain to you. When a difficult situation arises, you won't have time to check this book for the right technique or the most effective phrases to use. You must have already learned the words, the attitude, and the techniques and made them part of your teaching style.

Use specific communication techniques for difficult situations.

The following communication skills will help you handle challenging situations. Learn these "how-tos" now, before you need them.

How to disarm criticism.

> "I do the best job I can for my students. So it's always hard when a parent criticizes my teaching or accuses me of not caring about a child. It hurts. All I can think about is defending myself."

One of the most distressing situations you may find yourself in as a teacher is to be on the receiving end of a barrage of criticism by a parent. It's usually unanticipated, generally uncomfortable, and almost always hurtful.

"You're the cause of my daughter's problem."

"If you knew what you were doing, my son wouldn't be in this mess."

"Your assignments are boring. Why would she want to study?"

"My son's never had problems before, so you must be doing something wrong."

Though comments like these may sting at first, don't become hurt or angry. Stay in control. Recognize that you're dealing with a very distraught parent and that you've got to keep a clear head. Maintain a professional attitude. *Don't* react in this way:

"Look, I'm doing the best job I can."

"I have 149 other students. I can't spend all of my time with your child."

"I've tried everything. You just don't realize how hard it is dealing with your child."

Reactionary statements like these are not the words of a confident professional. They inspire neither respect nor understanding from the parent. Defensive responses such as these will not help you break down a parent's anger. They only shut down communication and leave the parent no choice but to continue his criticism. And once this cycle begins, it's hard to break.

You need to know how to quickly disarm the criticism and get the parent back on a more productive track.

Follow these guidelines.

If the parent's concern and criticism are justified, accept your mistake.

Sometimes parents are justified in their criticism. Teachers, like anyone else, can make a mistake. It's difficult, however, in the face of an angry tirade, to sit back and think, "Wait a minute, maybe there's some truth to what this parent is saying." You have to take this step, though, if you are to turn a confrontation into a more positive relationship. Stop, think, and then answer the parent honestly and straightforwardly. Don't make excuses or place blame on others. Make your statement clearly.

"You have reason to be angry. I should have contacted you sooner about this problem."

"I feel you are right to be upset. I should not have become so angry with your son the other day."

"You have reason to be frustrated. I was unaware that your child had a problem with this subject, and I should have been."

Admitting your mistakes may make you feel uneasy, but just think about the effect your words can have on the parent. Your response may defuse the parent's pent-up anger and resentment and pave the way for further constructive communication.

If the criticism is incorrect, or only partially correct, follow these steps:

1. **Listen to the parent's complaints without defending or justifying yourself.** The parent is angry and needs to talk. Give her the chance to "let it out." Use the effective communication skills introduced in Chapter 9. Watch your body language and make sure it reflects openness rather than defensiveness. Look at the parent while she is speaking and make it clear that you are paying attention to what is being said. Let the parent vent her anger or frustration, and show that you understand her point of view by using reflective listening techniques.

2. **Show your empathy and concern by asking the parent for more specific information about the complaint.**
This is the most useful way to disarm a parent's criticism. By asking questions, you are showing that you care about what the parent is saying. In addition, you are showing that you are able to handle criticism and maintain control in the conversation.

"That really concerns me. Can you explain more about what you mean?"

"Can you give me some examples of what you are saying?"

"Have I done something like this before?"

Remember that, justified or not, the parent's anger is real. People who are angry need to feel that they are being listened to. Let the parent talk it out.

3. **Now refocus the conversation. Restate the problem behavior and clarify why it is not in the student's best interests to act this way.**
After listening, you must refocus the conversation on the child's behavior and move away from the parent's criticism.

"I understand how upset you are, but we still must help your child get his work done so that he won't fall behind."

"I hear your point, but your daughter must do her homework or her grades will drop."

"I can see how frustrated you are with the situation, but we must help your son stop his disruptive behavior in class so that he doesn't continue to get into trouble."

4. **If a parent is still critical or angry, point out that conflict between the two of you is harmful to the student.**
Be a peacemaker. Explain that continued antagonism is not in anyone's best interests, especially the child's.

"I hear your point, but our disagreeing will only harm Stuart and will not help him solve his problem."

"You have a right to be upset with me, but this won't help Tom."

"I know we don't see eye to eye on this issue, but we can't help Juliette unless we work together."

5. **Finally, if the parent is still upset, suggest that he talk with the principal.**
Do not allow a critical parent to continue criticizing you. If it becomes clear that the parent is not going to calm down, it is appropriate to have the parent talk to the principal. Just bringing up this alternative may calm down the parent.

"It seems as though you and I cannot resolve this issue, so maybe you should speak with the principal about it."

This kind of dialogue can disarm criticism.
Here is a conversation between a parent and a teacher who uses the techniques described to disarm the parent's criticism.

Teacher: I'm concerned about Ted's fighting. He's had three fights with other students in the last three days.

Parent: He says the other kids pick on him and you don't do anything about it.

Teacher: *(listen, nodding head)* Uh-huh.

Parent: It's just not right. He's never had problems in school before. I just don't know what's going on in your class.

Teacher: *(ask for more information while, if appropriate, leaning forward)* Can you tell me more of what he says about how the kids pick on him?

Parent:	He says Milo and Kevin tease him. He says sometimes you're standing right there and you don't do anything.
Teacher:	*(avoid defensiveness in your body language—don't cross your arms, don't lean backward)* Are there any other problems he's had with students that he's told you about where he felt that I did nothing?
Parent:	He said the same thing happened last week with Jeremy.
Teacher:	Mr. Cole, I can understand why you would be upset if you were told he was being picked on and I watched and did nothing. I do not allow students to pick on one another. I would never condone this behavior by ignoring it. But we really have to discuss ways to help Ted stop fighting. We both want what's best for him, and if we work together, we can make that happen.

How to keep the parent conference focused on your goals.

"I feel prepared when I begin a conference, but with some parents it just seems to fall apart. Usually these are parents who have something to complain about. When the conference is over, they've said it all and I'm left thinking about what I didn't get a chance to say."

Too often, teachers lose control of a conference to a parent who takes over the agenda. Staying in control of a conference means keeping parents focused on your goals. This can be difficult when parents are upset or anxious. They may want to talk about the student's other problems, problems at home, or excuses for why the student is behaving inappropriately. When teachers get sidetracked and allow the parent's goals to divert the conference in a nonproductive direction, little is accomplished.

We will look at two very effective techniques for keeping a conference focused on your objectives. The broken-record and the wrong-person techniques are very effective for keeping a conference in focus. Both techniques can be used in a variety of situations that demand attention be paid to the issue at hand.

Bear in mind that neither the broken-record nor the wrong-person technique should be used in situations in which the parent honestly tries to help solve the problem by offering comments from his own perspective. Do not stifle or cut off communication. Always hear a parent out before you decide whether his concern may be legitimate or just an attempt to change the subject or place blame.

Use the broken-record technique.

You can keep from getting sidetracked by using the broken-record technique. When you use this technique, keep repeating your goals for the conference again and again, like a broken record.

Here's how it's done.

Clearly communicate to the parent that you understand her concerns and goals. Then restate your goal for the conference.

> *Parent:* I wish somebody at this school would do something about the way the other kids are acting at recess. Every day, Ron comes home telling me about how all the kids are getting him mad and making him get into fights.
>
> *Teacher:* *(indicate that you understand the parent's concern)* Mrs. Evans, I understand you feel that the other children are picking on your son, but *(restate the goal)* **we need to focus on how we can work together to help your son stop fighting at school.**

If the parent continues to focus on different goals, or argues with you, keep repeating your goal without being sidetracked by the parent's comments.

> *Parent:* But he comes home every day upset about what the other kids say. I want something to be done about this.
>
> *Teacher:* I understand your concern about your child being picked on, but *(use the broken record)* **we must focus on how we can stop him from fighting in school.**
>
> *Parent:* But he always says it's not his fault. Like I've told you, the kids won't leave him alone.
>
> *Teacher:* At a later time we can discuss the children picking on your son. I understand how concerned you are about that. But our time here today is limited, and *(use the broken record)* **we must discuss how we can help him stop fighting in school.**

When you use the broken-record technique, you are showing the parent not only that you recognize her concern but that you have enough control and confidence to redirect the conference to the problem at hand.

Use the wrong-person technique.

Some parents will try to shift the responsibility for their child's poor behavior onto a teacher's shoulders. They will make it seem as though you, rather than the student, are the one causing the problem. The wrong-person technique can help the parent focus on the real situation. When using this technique, take great care not to sound hostile. Don't put the parent down. Keep your mind on the golden rule and speak to the parent in the manner in which you would like to be spoken to if the situation were reversed.

Here are two examples.

Teacher: If Evan chooses to continue to misbehave, I will be forced to keep him after school.

Parent: Wait just a minute. You can't do that. If you keep him after school, he'll miss the bus. Then I'll have to leave work to pick him up. If I don't work, I don't get paid.

Teacher: Mr. Curtis, **I think you're talking to the wrong person**. If you don't want to miss work, you'll have to talk to Evan about that. If he adjusts his behavior, he won't have to stay after school.

Teacher: Kristin broke a class rule three times today. That means she will have to stay 15 minutes after school tomorrow.

Parent: I'm sorry, but you can't have Kristin stay late tomorrow. She has soccer practice.

Teacher: Mrs. Kelly, **I think you're talking to the wrong person**. If Kristin does not want to stay after school, she will have to learn to follow the school rules. Otherwise, I have no choice but to keep her after school.

As mentioned before, neither the broken-record nor the wrong-person technique is meant to shut down the lines of communication. In fact, it is extremely important that you always invite, listen to, and, if appropriate, accept a parent's input.

How to get a commitment from noncooperative parents.

Getting support from a noncooperative parent may depend on more than disarming criticism or keeping the conversation focused. At some point, you will have to get a commitment from the parent to support you. This can be difficult, especially when the parent is still angry, upset, or overwhelmed.

There are specific steps you can take to motivate these parents to support you. You need to let parents know

■ why it is in their child's best interest that they support you;

■ why you, as a teacher, cannot handle a problem on your own;

■ what the outcome will be for the child if the parent does not work with you.

Here's what to do:

1. **Emphasize that you cannot solve the child's problem on your own.**
    You must clearly explain to the parent that you are limited in your ability to motivate her child to improve behavior or classroom performance. Parents must understand that the greatest power to affect change lies with them.

    "I want to be very clear with you. As a teacher, there is only so much I can do to motivate your child to behave at school. I can promise you that I will do everything in my power to help your child. But you must understand that you are really the one(s) who can make the difference.

2. **Point out that the parent is the most influential person in a child's life.**
    Stress to parents that they are truly the most important people in their child's life.

    "You are the most important person in your child's life. What you say to your child and what you expect of him make a tremendous difference in how he looks at himself. You have the ability to turn things around for your child. But to do that you must be willing to support my efforts here at school."

3. **Present the negative outcome you feel will occur if the parent does not support you.**
    Sometimes you have to lay it on the line. A parent who won't get involved is jeopardizing the child's success in school—and needs to know what that can mean. Too often, teachers avoid letting parents know the potential negative consequences of their uninvolvement.

Here are some typical problems students have, and the potential short-term and long-term negative outcomes.

Problem: The student will not do homework.
Short-term negative outcomes:
The student will fall behind in class.
The student will fail tests.
The student will earn poor grades.
Long-term negative outcomes:
The student may be held back in school.
The student will never reach academic potential.
The student has greater potential for dropping out of school.

Problem: The student fights with peers.
Short-term negative outcomes:
The student will continue to receive detention at school.
The student will have fewer and fewer friends.
The student will face suspension.
Long-term negative outcomes:
The student's self-esteem will decrease.
The student will never learn to deal appropriately with conflict.
The student will face the real possibility of expulsion later.
The student will not get along with coworkers as an adult.

Problem: The student is chronically tardy or truant.
Short-term negative outcomes:
The student will fall behind academically.
The student may eventually be suspended.
Long-term negative outcomes:
The student may be held back.
The student may eventually drop out of school.

If necessary, here's what to say to parents.

"It's my responsibility to tell you what you can expect to happen if you don't support my efforts to help your child. Your child is not turning in any homework assignments or classroom assignments. Because he's not doing his work, he's not keeping up in class and he's failing his tests. Unless the situation changes, he will fail this subject. And that means a strong possibility of being held back next year.

"Mrs. Rey, those are just the short-term consequences he faces. I must also tell you that students who are held back for these reasons run a much greater risk of ultimately dropping out of school. And the long-term consequences of that are loss of self-esteem, poorer choices of jobs, and a life that just isn't as full of promise as it could have been."

Only present the negative picture of the consequences of uninvolved parenting if all else fails. Usually it is best to approach a reluctant parent with drawing the positive picture that you will create together if the parent gets involved and supports your efforts to help the child at school.

How to deal with a parent who makes an unscheduled visit to school.

"I was standing in front of the class, giving a social studies lecture, when this parent roared through the door demanding that I talk to him right then and there. He was obviously ready to explode. I wasn't sure what to do."

Few incidents are as upsetting as having a parent barge into your classroom or stop you in the hall on the way to class demanding to discuss an issue with you on the spot. You are caught off guard, students are present, and the parent may be angry and impatient. This is a situation that you must handle skillfully, otherwise it may escalate and become extremely unpleasant for you, the parent, and the student(s).

Here are some very simple techniques to use when handling these situations:

1. **First, be sensitive to the parent's concerns.**
   Keep this in mind: No matter how inappropriate a parent's behavior may be, he obviously must be upset or anxious to have come to school in this manner. If at all possible, stop what you are doing and listen. Put yourself in the parent's place. Be sensitive to what he is saying.

   "Mr. Santiago, you must be very upset to come here today to talk to me."

   "Mrs. Burke, I can see that you are very worried about Tracy's grades, or you wouldn't be coming to school like this."

2. **Let the parent know that his concerns are too important to discuss at this time.**
   Defuse the parent's anger. Let him know that you, too, want to discuss the problem, but that you would prefer to schedule a meeting at a time that is more conducive to finding a solution.

"I hear how upset you are about Paul's suspension. This issue is too important to discuss now when I've got 25 students here. We need to find a time when we can discuss it in more detail."

"I hear how upset you are with how I dealt with your daughter. This is too important to discuss now when I have to be in class in two minutes. We need to find a time when we can meet and talk."

3. **Set a time with the parent to talk about the problem.**

   Be very careful not to let the parent feel that you're putting her off. Assure the parent that you want to discuss the issue further. Tell the parent exactly when she can expect to hear from you.

   "I will call you as soon as school is over today and we can discuss it further."

   "Could you please wait for me in the office? I have a break in 15 minutes. I'd like to talk to you about setting a time when we can meet."

   "I will call you at home tonight. We'll make an appointment to get together and discuss this problem."

4. **If necessary, get administrative help.**

   If the previously mentioned techniques do not work, and the parent stays in the classroom or continues to follow you through the halls, get help from the principal or vice principal immediately. If necessary, give a note to a student to take to the office asking for assistance. This is especially important if a parent seems out of control and threatens you in any way. Under no circumstances should you stand there and allow a parent to verbally abuse or threaten you.

Here's a sample conversation with a parent who makes an unscheduled visit.

Below is an example of a teacher dealing effectively with an angry parent who has made an unscheduled visit to school.

The teacher is walking in the hall on her way to class.

Parent: Mrs. Shelby, I want to speak with you right now. How in the _____ can you suspend my daughter? What is your problem?

Teacher: Mrs. Webster, can you explain what you mean?

Parent:	Yes, I can explain what I mean. You sent Denise home. I had to leave work. I really can't believe this. You are on my kid's case every single day. I've had it with you and this school.
Teacher:	You seem very angry and upset.
Parent:	You're right about that. I've had it.
Teacher:	Mrs. Webster, this issue is too important for us to discuss now. I'm on my way to class. I want to talk to you about this in greater detail, but we'll have to talk later.
Parent:	I want to talk about it now.
Teacher:	I understand, Mrs. Webster, but this is much too important for us to discuss now. I will call you as soon as school is out today at 3:30. Will you be home?
Parent:	Well, I won't be home. I have to go to work and make up the time I've lost because you suspended Denise.
Teacher:	Then can I call you at work?
Parent:	No, you know you can't call me at work. I'm in enough trouble there already.
Teacher:	Then what time do you get home from work?
Parent:	About 7:00.
Teacher:	Then I'll call your home tonight at 7:30.
Parent:	You'd better do that!
Teacher:	I promise I will call you at 7:30 tonight. I hear how upset you are and I want to help Denise as much as you do.

How to handle phone calls from parents.

"It's one thing for me to make the phone call to a parent. I can prepare myself and take charge of the conversation. It's a lot harder when I get a message that a parent wants me to call him. I may not know what the parent is concerned or upset about. I have to be ready for anything."

You've learned how to structure a conversation when you call a parent about a problem. But what happens when the parent calls you? Obviously, you can't plan exactly what you will say. Every phone call from a parent is different. You can, however, be prepared to handle the parent's emotional state as well as take steps toward solving the problem.

Here are some guidelines to follow.

1. **Listen to what the parent has to say.**

   If a parent calls you, she is concerned about something. At the beginning of the conversation, just listen to what the parent has to say. Don't interrupt or try to cut the parent's comments short. Listen carefully and take notes.

2. **Be sensitive to the parent's concerns.**

   You may feel that the parent is overreacting to something. You may feel that she is being overly protective. You may even feel that the parent is being manipulated by the child. That doesn't matter. What does matter is that you make sure that anything you say reflects an awareness of the parent's emotional state and her concerns about this issue. Under no circumstances should you make value judgments. For example, never say "It's ridiculous for you to be upset," or "There's no reason for you to be concerned." Comments like these will alienate the parent and hinder further productive conversation.

3. **Use "disarming criticism" techniques if necessary.**

   Review the techniques described earlier in this chapter. These techniques can be used just as effectively in a phone conversation as in a face-to-face conference. Listen to the parent's concerns, ask for more information, and be empathetic to her feelings. Under no circumstances should you become defensive, try to blame the student, or tell the parent she is wrong in calling. Handle the situation well and you may open the door to future positive communication with this parent.

4. **If you did something wrong, apologize.**

   If the parent has a legitimate concern, the best technique is to simply apologize for making a mistake. Don't become defensive. Don't minimize your actions. Apologize clearly to the parent and reassure her that such actions will not occur again.

5. **If the parent is misinformed, point out the facts.**

   Sometimes a parent may call because of something the child says about your classroom, your teaching, or other students. The student's reporting may be inaccurate, but it is still very important that you listen to the parent's concerns before gently but firmly pointing out the truth.

"Mrs. Debs, I understand that Cleavon told you he has been given five worksheets to do in 10 minutes and that there's no way he can finish them on time. The truth is, Mrs. Debs, that he, and the other students, have been given two worksheets that can easily be done in the time allowed if the students stick to their work."

"Mr. Lombardi, I understand that Benjamin said he was singled out and embarrassed in front of the whole class. I understand that he may feel that way, but here is what happened. He was shouting in class. I walked over to him and, very quietly and privately, told him that he had a choice to either stop shouting or sit away from the other children. He continued to shout, and so he was told to sit in the time-out spot."

6. **Do not make quick decisions.**
   When a parent is upset, she is likely to want you to make a quick decision to change something: your discipline methods, your teaching methods, your curriculum, your classroom organization, etc. Unless you agree that the particular situation warrants immediate action, do not allow the parent to pressure you into making changes before you've carefully thought them through. Let the parent know you hear what she is saying and you understand the concern, but that you want to think about the situation before taking any action.

   "Mrs. Rogers, I hear what you are saying about changing Stephanie's reading group. I want to give this situation some thought. I will call you tomorrow to discuss it further."

   "Mr. Ikura, I understand you want Greg's seat changed. There's some merit to what you are saying. I want to think about the effect it would have on him, and I will talk to you about it tomorrow."

7. **If appropriate, ask the parent to come in for a conference.**
   If a parent raises an issue that cannot be easily resolved in a brief phone conversation, ask her to come in for a conference to discuss it further. This will communicate to the parent your concern and interest in what she has to say.

8. **Admit you do not have all the answers.**
   If the parent raises an issue regarding a student's academic performance or behavior that you do not have an answer for, do not hesitate to say so. You don't have to pretend to know everything. However, you should reassure the

parent that you understand her concern and will look into the matter further. For example:

"I hear what you are saying. I do not have an answer, but I will meet with the *(principal/psychologist/counselor)*, and I will contact you again with some information that can help your daughter."

"I hear what you are saying. I do not have an answer, but I will speak with the director of the after-school care program and get back to you with some ideas for helping your son."

9. **Thank the parent for calling.**
   Whatever the nature of the conversation, let the parent know that you appreciate the fact that she called. Try to end the conversation on as positive a note as possible.

   "Thank you for bringing this to my attention. I will look into it and call you with a response tomorrow."

   "I understand that this is a difficult situation. I appreciate your telling me how you feel about it."

Use specialized techniques with the most difficult parents.

"I have one parent this year that I can't seem to reach, no matter what I do. She avoids me, won't answer my calls, and when I do get hold of her, she makes it clear that she wants nothing to do with me or the school. Unfortunately, her son is on his way to losing it all. I can't let that happen—not until I've tried everything I possibly can."

The ideas, suggestions, and techniques presented in *Parents on Your Side* will enable you to get 98 percent of parents on your side. The remaining 2 percent are the hardest of all to handle. You may need to employ additional techniques if you are to have any chance of successfully reaching these parents.

NOTE: The methods presented in this chapter should only be used with administrative support.

Method 1:
Take the child home or to the parent's place of work.

If calling the parent doesn't produce results, try doing what the principal did in the following situation:

> George Cotter was the classic fifth grade troublemaker. He had been a problem since he had transferred to the school at the beginning of the year. His father refused to cooperate when contacted by George's teacher.
>
> One day, George threw a chair across the room and missed hitting the head of a fellow student by three inches. The principal, Mrs. Burns, was notified. George was removed from class and suspension proceedings began. The principal phoned Mr. Cotter at work. She spoke first to his supervisor, who said Mr. Cotter couldn't come to the phone. Mrs. Burns would not be put off. She told the supervisor that there was an emergency at his son's school. Mr. Cotter came to the phone within two minutes.

Here is the conversation that ensued.

Principal:	Mr. Cotter, this is Mrs. Burns, the principal at George's school. Your son was involved in a serious incident today. We need you to come to school immediately and help us work out this problem.
Mr. Cotter:	Hey, why are you calling me at work for something like that? I can't come to school now. I've got to work for five more hours.
Principal:	When your son causes problems during our working day, you will have to leave your job and help us solve the problem.
Mr. Cotter:	I can't do that. If I leave the office now, they'll dock my pay.
Principal:	Mr. Cotter, you're talking to the wrong person. Every time George chooses to disrupt his class, I'll have to call you and ask you to take him home. If you don't want to be called, I suggest you talk to him about following the rules. He's becoming a serious problem, and the school can no longer be responsible for him.
Mr. Cotter:	Wait a minute. That kid is your problem from nine to three.
Principal:	No, Mr. Cotter. George is your responsibility 24 hours a day. You have a choice. Either you come to school now, or I'll be forced to bring George to you.

Mr. Cotter: Very funny. I'm not leaving work, and I don't want you to call me here ever again.

Principal: You leave me no choice. Good-bye, Mr. Cotter.

The principal took care of some last-minute details, ushered George to her car, and drove to the father's place of employment. It was a long drive, about 10 miles away, but Mrs. Burns was determined to solve the problem of George's behavior once and for all.

Mrs. Burns took George into the manager's office, explained the situation to him, and Mr. Cotter was summoned. Seeing his son and Mrs. Burns standing next to his angry manager was very upsetting to Mr. Cotter. He had no choice. He took his son home and lost a day's pay.

The father in this situation was so greatly inconvenienced that he realized the teacher and principal meant business, and he finally agreed to work with the school to change his son's behavior. At a meeting with the parent, teacher, and principal, a contract was formulated to improve George's behavior. Mr. Cotter agreed to provide discipline whenever he received notice that his son was disruptive in school. Rewards for good reports were also agreed upon. The principal, teacher, parent, and student all signed the contract. In addition, the school arranged for regular meetings between George and the guidance counselor. Within three weeks, the problem was solved.

> NOTE: Whenever you need to take severe measures such as this to ensure parental support, have the guidance counselor follow up on the home situation. There is always the possibility that the child may be physically or mentally abused. Report any suspicion of child abuse to the proper authorities.

Method 2:
Have the parent monitor student behavior at school.

Some parents simply will not believe their child is a serious problem at school. Others absolutely refuse to do anything about it. In these cases, offer parents a choice—either they come to school and monitor their child, or the school will have to suspend the child. If the parent agrees, have her sit in on every class with the student, including cafeteria and gym. (Note: Use this method with older students only. Younger students may find having Mom or Dad in class pleasurable.)

To have its greatest effect, the parent must continue coming to school until the student shows improvement or the parent agrees to help.

This method is successful because

- the parent sees exactly how the student behaves in school;

- the parent is usually inconvenienced and eventually agrees to help;

- the student feels pressure from peers about having her parent at school and begins to behave.

Method 3:
Detain students after school and have parents sign them out.

A frequently used corrective action for students who severely misbehave is to detain them after school. Then, when the detention period ends, the parent is required to come to school to sign the student out. A parent who has to leave work to pick up his child may be inconvenienced enough to work with the school to improve the child's behavior. Always give parents 24 hours notice before using this method.

Method 4:
Have parents escort truant students to school.

If a student is continually truant and the parent has not cooperated in solving the problem, offer a choice. The parent must bring the child to school each morning and sign him in, or the child will be suspended.

Method 5:
Visit the student's home.

A home visit is an effective positive technique to use with parents. Going to a student's home to deliver good news or get acquainted with parents is one of the best means at your disposal to demonstrate that you care about a student and her success. A home visit is also a powerful technique to use with parents you are having trouble reaching or dealing with. A home visit gives you the opportunity to sit down with a parent in his own home and discuss the problem at hand. The visit shows the parent you care enough to go out of your way to solve a problem. The visit shows that you mean business.

Follow these guidelines:

1. Do not arrive at a student's home unannounced. Make every effort to set up an appointment. Ask your administrator for help if you are unable to reach the parent.

2. As with any other conference, be prepared. Write down all points you wish to cover with the parent and bring your notes and documentation with you.

3. Review guidelines for disarming criticism and keeping a conference focused on your goals.

4. Keep a positive and professional attitude. Listen carefully to the parent's concerns and be sensitive to what he says.

5. At the end of the visit, let the parent know that there will be follow-up contact from you. Once having made this effort, you will want to do all you can to keep this parent involved.

Difficult situations *can* be handled successfully.

Dealing with difficult parents may be unsettling, but when situations are handled with skill and confidence, you can move toward a productive outcome. As was stated at the beginning of this chapter, these situations are the ones that will really test your professionalism and confidence.

If you speak and act with confidence, if you've learned to recognize and deal with your own roadblocks, if you've practiced and honed your own communication skills so you can recognize and move parents past their roadblocks, then you have indeed achieved the ability to handle difficult situations with parents. Getting even reluctant parents on your side will greatly improve your students' chances for success.

Dealing with Difficult Situations
REMINDERS

DO

➤ Make sure you learn and review the techniques of this chapter frequently to make sure you have them at hand when the need arises. Preparation is key.

➤ Always show respect, practice sensitivity, and above all, listen to the parents' concerns.

➤ Disarm criticism.

➤ Keep conferences focused by using the broken-record and wrong-person techniques.

➤ Get commitment of reluctant parents by impressing upon them how important their involvement is to their child's success.

DON'T

➤ Don't be defensive when facing a parent's criticism. If it's valid, apologize and adjust your behavior accordingly. If it's not, gently explain your rationale to the parent and move her toward commitment to changing the child's behavior.

➤ Don't allow a parent to corner you in the hallway or during a class. If a parent is upset, set a time that's more appropriate for discussing the problem.

➤ Don't make rash on-the-spot decisions. Always allow time for you to think about the best course of action.

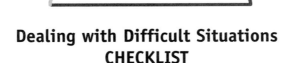

Dealing with Difficult Situations CHECKLIST

Have you:

___ learned and thoroughly reviewed the guidelines regarding dealing with difficult situations?

___ reviewed the communication skills presented in Chapter 9?

___ discussed with the administration which procedures to follow should a parent come to school and abuse or threaten you?

___ made sure you've done everything in your power to help a student adjust his behavior, so it won't ever escalate to a difficult situation?

Conclusion:
Ending the Year on a Positive Note

Throughout this book, we have presented many techniques to help you implement a positive parent involvement plan that will carry you successfully from the first day of school to the last. The end of the year is the time to put it all together and take those final steps that will put the finishing touches on a noteworthy school experience.

This chapter will show you how to take the opportunity to make final, meaningful contact with parents and students. You will learn how to do the following:

- Provide a positive conclusion to the school year.

- Take pride in a job well done.

Keep in mind that you're not just ending one year; you're opening the door for all the years ahead. The effects of everything you've done this year are cumulative. The roadblocks you've cleared won't be roadblocks to the next teacher. What a step forward that is for everyone.

Provide a positive conclusion to the school year.

What you do as the year comes to a close will ensure that your students and their parents move forward with the best possible attitude toward school, education, and teachers. Don't let your involvement with parents slide during this period. Carry through with the professionalism and care you have demonstrated all year long.

Make Open House a parent thank-you event.

Just as Back-to-School Night set the stage for a year of dynamic parent involvement, Open House in the spring can serve as a retrospective of all that's been accomplished. Traditionally, Open House is a time for parents to tour the classroom with their children, look at their work, and chat amiably with the teacher and other parents. Now that you have parents on your side, it's time to add a new component: a heartfelt thanks to parents for their support.

Let "Thanks to you, it's been a great year" be your theme. Carry it through on the invitations you send home and on signs or banners you place in the classroom. Have students write notes to parents thanking them for all their help. At Open House, present parents with small thank-you favors.

- Have a basket of apples by the door with a sign that reads, "An apple from the teacher to the best team of parents ever!"

- Have a friend serve as photographer and take an instant photo of each parent and child. Slip each photo into a construction paper frame that says, "Thanks to you, it's been a great year."

Above all, make sure every parent leaves with the knowledge that his help has been noticed, appreciated, and worthwhile.

Send end-of-the-year notes to students.

"It was 25 years ago, but I still remember the note my teacher Mr. O'Leary wrote to me. It made me feel terrific. Finally, after all was said and done, I knew he thought well of me, and that meant a lot. As a matter of fact, I still have that note somewhere."

— Parent

Your words can have a lasting effect on students of any age. At the end of the year, take the time to give your students the gift of a few thoughtfully chosen sentences.

Don't view this correspondence as a perfunctory duty. Get excited about it. You are launching your students into their future. Fuel their journey with the best, most encouraging words you can. Chances are, if you were able to look ahead 25 years, you'd find some of your messages tucked away in boxes and drawers. And that speaks volumes about how the child felt when he received it.

"My seven-year-old daughter came running into the house waving a letter addressed to her. She kept shouting, 'It's from Mrs. Montoya! It's from Mrs. Montoya!' And that's just what it was—a letter from her teacher four weeks after school was out. You should have seen the smile on her face. She must have read and reread that letter a dozen times. Now it's pinned up on her bulletin board."

— Parent

Sample End-of-the-Year Notes to Students

> Roberto:
>
> I've watched you work hard this year to achieve your goals. I know it hasn't been easy, but you have succeeded admirably. I am proud of you, and I am proud to have been your teacher.
>
> Sincerely,
>
> Mr. Gonzales

> Dear Jessica,
>
> Thank you for all the things you did this year that made life in Room 9 so pleasant. I love the big picture and the poem you gave me. It will always remind me of the fun we had planning our model community. You were such a responsible mayor!
>
> You are a talented and creative artist, Jessica, and a hardworking student. It has been my pleasure to have been your teacher.
>
> Your friend,
>
> Miss Walker

Send thank-you notes to parents.

You've enlisted their support all year long. Now let them know how valuable their involvement and interest have been. This final contact from you is exceedingly important. Remember that this parent will be a parent in someone else's class next year. Do everything you can to pass along a group of parents who feel that their involvement was appreciated and who are eager to continue that involvement.

Sample End-of-the-Year Notes to Parents

Dear Mrs. Marcum:

This year has been especially successful for Jeff. I hope you realize what a big part you've played in that success. Once Jeff began doing his homework assignments, he found that he could keep up with class discussions and do better on tests. You've seen the results on his report card. Thanks again for giving him the message that homework must be done! Hope your summer is terrific.

Sincerely,

Mr. Amaral

Dear Mr. and Mrs. Avery:

It's hard to believe this terrific year has ended. I have so enjoyed working with both of you. You've been generous with your time and expertise. Our World Bazaar wouldn't have been the same without the wonderful posters you painted for us. Have a wonderful summer. I look forward to seeing you at school events next year.

Sincerely,

Mrs. Pollard

Call parents with whom you've worked to solve specific problems.

Take a moment at the end of the year to think about those parents with whom you've worked to solve specific problems. These parents deserve an extra-special pat on the back for the efforts they have made on behalf of their children. Make sure they get recognition from you. Review the progress made throughout the year. If appropriate, give guidelines for continued success. Above all, thank these parents for working with you to solve their children's problems. Point out the difference their supportive involvement made.

Take pride in a job well done.

You have set a new standard in education. Through your conscientious efforts to form a partnership with parents, you have demonstrated that quality education is a shared responsibility. You have taken the lead with confidence and professionalism. Be proud of your accomplishments. Know that the parents and students you have worked with will move ahead with a more positive attitude toward education. You have made a difference in the lives of your students and their parents.

You are an effective teacher.

Ending the Year on a Positive Note
REMINDERS

DO

➤ Make Open House a thank-you event.

➤ Send end-of-the year notes to parents and students.

➤ Call parents you worked with regarding specific problems.

➤ Use the end of the year to further a positive relationship with students and parents that will last for years to come.

DON'T

➤ Don't underestimate the importance of a simple thank-you.

➤ Don't underestimate the work you've done to create a good relationship with parents. It is important to other teachers as well.

Ending the Year on a Positive Note CHECKLIST

Have you:

____ thanked all parents who helped you throughout the year?

____ sent a note to parents who didn't attend Open House?

____ called parents who helped you with specific problems?

____ sent a special note to each student?

Recommended Reading and Bibliography

Barth, R. (1979). Home-based reinforcement of school behavior: A review and analysis. *Review of Educational Research, 49*(3), 436–458.

Bridgman, A. (1985, February 6). States launching barrage of initiatives, survey finds. *Education Week,* 11–29.

Bronfenbrenner, Urie. (1966). *A report on longitudinal evaluations of pre-school programs.* Washington, DC: Department of Health, Education and Welfare.

Brookover, W. B., & Gigliotti, R. J. (1988). *First teachers: Parental involvement in the public schools.* Alexandria, VA: National School Boards Association.

Bumstead, R. A. (1982, March). Public or private? What parents want from their schools. *Principal,* 39–43.

Canter, L., & Canter, M. (1985). *Assertive discipline resource materials workbook.* Santa Monica, CA: Lee Canter & Associates.

Canter, L., & Canter, M. (1988). *Assertive discipline for parents.* New York, NY: Harper & Row.

Canter, L., & Canter, M. (2001). *Assertive discipline: Positive behavior management for today's classroom.* Los Angeles, CA: Canter & Associates.

Canter, L., & Hausner, L., Ph.D. (1987). *Homework without tears.* New York, NY: Harper & Row.

Caplan, N., Whitmore, J., Bui, Q., & Trautmann, M. (1985). *Scholastic achievement among the children of Southeast Asian refugees.* Ann Arbor, MD: Institute for Social Research.

Cavarretta, J. (1998, May). Parents are a school's best friend. *Educational Leadership, 55*(8), 12–15.

Chavkin, N. F. (1998, Spring/Summer). Making the case for school, family, and community partnerships: Recommendations for research. *School Community Journal, 8*(1), 9–21.

Chavkin, N. F., & Williams, D. L., Jr. (1988). Critical issues in teacher training for parent involvement in education. *Journal of Sociology & Social Welfare,* 17–28.

Chavkin, N. F., & Williams, D. L., Jr. (1989, October). Essential elements of strong parent involvement programs. *Educational Leadership,* 18–20.

Chira, S. (1993, June 23). What do teachers want most? Help from parents. *The New York Times,* p. 7.

Clapp, B. (1989). The discipline challenge. *Instructor, XCIX*(2), 32–34.

Coleman, J., & others. (1966). *Equality of educational opportunity.* Washington, DC: Office of Education.

Collins, C. H., Moles, O. C., & Cross, M. (1982). *The home-school connection: Selected partnership programs in large cities.* Boston, MA: Institute for Responsive Education.

Epstein, J. L. (1993). *Effects on parents of teacher practices in parental involvement.* Baltimore, MD: Johns Hopkins University Center for Social Organization of Schools.

Epstein, J. L. (1995, May). School/family/community partnerships: Caring for the children we share. *Phi Delta Kappan, 76*(9), 701–712.

Epstein, J. L. (1996). Advances in family, community, and school partnerships. *New Schools, New Communities, 12*(3), 5–13.

Epstein, J. L. (1997, September/October). Six types of school-family-community involvement. *Harvard Education Letter.* [Online]. Available: http://www.edletter.org/past/issues/1997-so/sixtypes.shtml.

Epstein, J. L. (1999). *Family partnerships with high schools: The parents' perspective.* [Research Report No. 32]. Baltimore, MD: Center for Research on the Education of Students Placed at Risk.

Farkas, S., & Johnson, J. (1999). Looking at the school: Public agenda asks African-American and white parents about their aspirations and their fears. *Arts Education Policy Review, 100*(4), 24–27.

Goodlad, J. I. (1982, May). An agenda for improving our schools. *Executive Review 2.*

Hanson, S. L., & Ginsburg, A. (1985). *Gaining ground: Values and high school success.* Washington, DC: U.S. Department of Education.

Harris, L. (Ed.). (1987). *The Metropolitan Life survey of the American teacher: Strengthening lines between home and school.* New York: Metropolitan Life Insurance Company.

Henderson, A. (1987). *The evidence continues to grow.* Columbia, MD: National Committee for Citizens in Education.

Henderson, A. (1995, March/April). Families and student achievement. *PTA Today, 20*(4), 12–14.

Herman, J., & Yeh, J. (1980). *Some effects of parent involvement in schools* (ED 206 963). Center for the Study of Evaluation, Graduate School of Education, University of California at Los Angeles.

Hewison, J. & Tizard, J. (1980). Parental involvement and reading attainment. *British Journal of Educational Psychology, 50,* 209–215.

Hispanic Policy Development Project. (1990). *Together is better.* New York: NY.

Institute for Responsive Education. (1982). *The home-school connection.* Boston: MA.

Institute for Responsive Education. (1990). *Equity and Choice, VI*(3). Boston: MA.

Kagan, S. L. (1984/1985). *Parent involvement research: A field in search of itself.* Boston, MA: Institute for Responsive Education.

Krasnow, J. (1990). *Building parent-teacher partnerships: Prospects for the perspective of the schools reaching out project.* Boston, MA: Institute for Responsive Education.

Langdon, C. A. (1996, November). The third Gallup/Phi Delta Kappa poll of teachers' attitudes toward the public schools. *Phi Delta Kappan, 78*(3), 244–250.

Langdon, C. A. (1997, November). The fourth Gallup/Phi Delta Kappa poll of teachers' attitudes toward the public schools. *Phi Delta Kappan, 79*(3), 212–220.

Lombana, J. H. (1983). *Home-school partnerships: Guidelines and strategies for the educator.* New York, NY: Grune & Stratton, Inc.

Lynn, L. (1997, September/October). Teaching teachers to work with families. *Harvard Education Letter.* [Online]. Available: http://www.edletter.org/past/issues/1997-so/teaching.shtml.

McAllister, S. S. (1990). *Parent involvement and success for all children: What we know now.* Boston, MA: Institute for Responsive Education.

McLaughlin, M., & Shields, P. (1987, October). Involving low-income parents in the schools: A role for policy? *Phi Delta Kappan,* 156–160.

McLaughlin, C. S., Ph.D. (1987). *Parent-teacher conferencing.* Springfield, IL: Charles C. Thomas.

Moles, O. C. (Ed.). (1996). *Reaching all families: Creating family-friendly schools.* Washington, DC: Office of Educational Research and Improvement.

National Center for Education Statistics. (Ed.). (1996). Types of contact between parents and school personnel. Indicator of the Month. Washington, DC: National Center for Education Statistics.

National Education Association. (1983). *Nationwide teacher opinion poll.* Washington, DC.

National School Boards Association. (1988). *First teachers: Parental involvement in the public schools.* Alexandria: VA.

Rich, D. (1987). *Teachers and parents: An adult-to-adult approach.* National Education Association of the United States. The Home and School Institute.

Rich, D. (1998). *Megaskills: How families can help children succeed in school and beyond.* Boston, MA: Houghton Mifflin Company.

Rich, D. (1995). Conference connections: How to make parent-teacher conferences a positive experience for all. *Instructor.*

Sanford, Dornbusch, et al. (1987). The relation of parenting style to adolescent school performance. *Child Development, 58,* 1244–1257.

Seeley, D. S. (1985). *Education through partnership.* Washington, DC: American Enterprise Institute for Public Policy Research.

Smith, M. B. (1968). School and home: Focus on achievement. *Developing Programs for Educationally Disadvantaged.* New York, NY: Teachers College Press.

Storer, J. H. (1995, Winter). Increasing parent and community involvement in schools: The importance of educators' beliefs. *Community Education Journal,* 16–19.

Thomas, W. B. (1980, November). Parental and community involvement: Rx for better school discipline. *Phi Delta Kappan,* 203–204.

United States Department of Education. (1986). *What works: Research about teaching and learning.* Washington, DC.

Walberg, H. (1984). Improving the productivity of America's schools. *Educational Leadership,* 41.

Welch, F. C., Ph.D., & Tisdale, P. C., Ph.D. (1986). *Between parent and teacher.* Springfield, IL: Charles C. Thomas.

Index

Make the Most of Your Professional Development Investment

Let Solution Tree (formerly National Educational Service) schedule time for you and your staff with leading practitioners in the areas of:

- **Professional Learning Communities** with Richard DuFour, Robert Eaker, Rebecca DuFour, and associates
- **Effective Schools** with associates of Larry Lezotte
- **Assessment *for* Learning** with Rick Stiggins and associates
- **Crisis Management and Response** with Cheri Lovre
- **Classroom Management** with Lee Canter and associates
- **Discipline With Dignity** with Richard Curwin and Allen Mendler
- **PASSport to Success** (parental involvement) with Vickie Burt
- **Peacemakers** (violence prevention) with Jeremy Shapiro

Additional presentations are available in the following areas:

- Youth at Risk Issues
- Bullying Prevention/Teasing and Harassment
- Team Building and Collaborative Teams
- Data Collection and Analysis
- Embracing Diversity
- Literacy Development
- Motivating Techniques for Staff and Students

Solution Tree

(formerly National Educational Service)
304 West Kirkwood Avenue
Bloomington, IN 47404-5131
(812) 336-7700
(800) 733-6786 (toll-free number)
FAX (812) 336-7790

NEED MORE COPIES OR ADDITIONAL RESOURCES ON THIS TOPIC?

Need more copies of this book? Want your own copy? Need additional resources on this topic? If so, you can order additional materials by using this form or by calling us toll free at (800) 733-6786 or (812) 336-7700. Or you can order by FAX at (812) 336-7790 or online at www.solution-tree.com.

Title	Price*	Qty	Total
Parents on Your Side® (K–8)	$ 19.95		
Parents on Your Side® Resource Materials Workbook (K–8)	11.95		
Classroom Management for Academic Success (K–12)	39.95		
First-Class Teacher (K–12)	22.95		
Assertive Discipline® (K–12)	19.95		
Assertive Discipline® Workbook (K–6)	11.95		
Assertive Discipline® Workbook (7–12)	11.95		
Assertive Discipline® Video Resource (K–6)	495.00		
Assertive Discipline® Video Resource (7–12)	495.00		
Succeeding With Difficult Students® (K–12)	17.95		
Succeeding With Difficult Students® Workbook (K–12)	11.95		
Succeeding With Difficult Students® Video Resource	495.00		
		SUBTOTAL	
		SHIPPING	
Continental U.S.: Please add 6% of order total. Outside continental U.S.: Please add 8% of order total.			
		HANDLING	
Continental U.S.: Please add $4. Outside continental U.S.: Please add $6.			
		TOTAL (U.S. funds)	

*Price subject to change without notice.

❏ Check enclosed   ❏ Purchase order enclosed
❏ Money order   ❏ VISA, MasterCard, Discover, or American Express (circle one)

Credit Card No._____ Exp. Date _____

Cardholder Signature _____

SHIP TO:

First Name_____ Last Name _____
Position _____
Institution Name _____
Address _____
City_____ State_____ ZIP _____
Phone_____ FAX _____
Email _____

Solution Tree (formerly National Educational Service)
304 West Kirkwood Avenue
Bloomington, IN 47404-5131
(812) 336-7700 • (800) 733-6786 (toll free)
FAX (812) 336-7790
email: orders@solution-tree.com
www.solution-tree.com